HOW TO

WRITE FOR
CHILDREN
AND
GET PUBLISHED

HOW TO

WRITE FOR CHILDREN

AND
GET PUBLISHED

LOUISE JORDAN

PIATKUS

The author would like to thank all those who have kindly given permission for their work to be included. Every effort has been made to correctly credit each extract. The publishers apologise for any error or omission and would be grateful to be notified of any correction that should be incorporated into the next edition of this book.

First published in 1998 by
Judy Piatkus (Publishers) Ltd
5 Windmill Street
London W1P 1HF

Reprinted 1998

The moral right of the author has been asserted

*A catalogue record for this book is available
from the British Library*

ISBN 0–7499–1702–4

Typeset by Phoenix Photosetting, Chatham, Kent
Printed and bound in Great Britain by
Biddles Ltd, Guildford and King's Lynn

CONTENTS

*with thanks to Iain Brown
for his editorial input*

INTRODUCTION

'Once upon a time' is no time, just as east of the sun and west of the moon, or the end of the world, is no place. In reality, however, it means 'at all times, in all places'. It is a declaration announcing that what you are going to hear is the truth – both in time and in space. And everyone, be he king or beggar, needs to hear the truth once in a while at least.

Erik Haugard on the writing of Hans Christian Andersen

Once upon a time . . .

Once upon a time, was – once – how all children's books started. Today they are more likely to start with first lines such as:

'Katie trudged over the dump'
(*Run, Zan, Run* by Catherine MacPhail)

'Maths exams! Ugh!'
(*Hacker* by Malorie Blackman)

'Every morning Filly and Fergal would wake up and wait for the arguments to start'
(*The Meteorite Spoon* by Philip Ridley)

'Jimmy Woods was the worst kind of bully'
(*Jimmy Woods and the Big Bad Wolf* by Mick Gowar)

"'Suppose,' said Lannie dreamily, "that you really could freeze somebody.'"

(Freeze Tag by Caroline B. Cooney)

If you hanker after the days of 'Once upon a Time', perhaps this book is not for you. If, on the other hand, you are gripped by power and immediacy of the first lines above and can sense excitement to come, read on.

WHY A CHILDREN'S BOOK?

'Everyone who has ever been a child, had a child, seen a child or heard a child thinks that he or she can write a children's book.'

So began a rather disparaging article on 'wannabe' children's writers in the *New York Times* a few years ago: the implication being that children's publishing should function as some sort of exclusive club where new members are all but barred.

Penguin Children's Books (which include Puffin) receive over 5000 unsolicited submissions every year. Out of this 'slush pile' (I hate that term!) maybe two or three are actually accepted for publication.

This isn't so discouraging when put in context. Even a relatively large children's publisher such as Penguin only publishes, in total, around 60 books a year; and you have to consider that most of these are either reprints, or commissions from already established authors, rather than new titles.

So children's publishing is a fairly exclusive club but, whilst new members may not be welcomed with open arms, they are certainly not blackballed. To gain membership, however, it is important to examine why you want to write a children's book in the first place.

Here are a few reasons that have been stated to me by would-be children's authors over the years:

'I really want to write an adult bestseller, but I thought I'd stand more chance with a children's book to start with.'
No! This must be the number one worst reason for choosing to write for children. For a start, writing a children's book is not *easier* than writing an adult book, merely *different*. Many potential children's writers feel that simplicity of vocabulary is the key:

it isn't. What *is* needed is a clarity of vision, and this is harder to achieve than you might think. Secondly, it is just as hard to get a children's book taken on by a publisher as it is to find a publisher for adult writing. Thirdly, you're never going to write a good children's book unless you are totally committed to the task in hand – unless you really *want* and *need* to write it.

'I want to make lots of money like Alan Ahlberg and Roald Dahl.'
No! Unless you make it to the very top, writing for children doesn't pay well. So don't give up the day job – not yet anyway.

'My children/nieces/nephews/grandchildren love my stories and say I should get them published.'
No! That is – 'No, that's not a good reason,' not – 'No, they don't like your stories.' They probably *do*, very much, but they're reacting to *you*, the person they love, as much as to the story itself. Don't get me wrong, it's a good starting point; it means that you can communicate successfully with children and hold their attention. Just remember that your children/nieces/ nephews/grandchildren aren't the public at large, neither are they publishers. To make the leap from storyteller extraordinaire to published writer is extremely tough. Keep hold of that first inspired spark – but let go of the stories themselves. Until you've finished reading this book, at any rate.

'There's nothing but rubbish published these days and I want to write the sort of books I used to enjoy as a child.'
Fine. Write the sort of books that you used to enjoy – but don't expect them to be published. Those books you enjoyed – the classics – *are* still being published, but if you think that anything more contemporary is rubbish then you haven't been looking in the right places. Anne Fine, Philip Ridley, Malorie Blackman, Robert Swindells, Chris Westwood . . . the list of wonderfully exciting and original authors goes on. Children's literature is scaling new heights from year to year.

'I've got a good idea.'
That certainly helps. A good idea is an essential starting point and a good idea which would only suit a young market is certainly a

WRITING BOOKS FOR CHILDREN

valid reason for writing specifically for children. Be warned though: is it *really* a good idea? Is it a book demanding to be born? Or have you got one eye on lucrative merchandising contracts and the other on potential television rights? If so, you probably haven't got a good idea at all. What you have got is a leaky business proposition which won't fool a children's publisher – or the children themselves.

'I want to write for me.'
Yes! It's as simple as that. The best children's writers are writing for themselves – not the child in themselves. Children's writer, Eleanor Farjeon, once advised would-be writers: 'Write only what *you* enjoy writing. Don't write down for children, don't try to be on their level, don't think there is a special tone they will respond to, don't be afraid of words or of things you feel children can't grasp. When you write for children, be yourself.'

Good advice. Writers may exploit emotions and thoughts remembered from their own childhood, but the stories they tell will be firmly entrenched in their own lives *today*.

'I want to pass on things that I have learned to the next generation.'
Yes – another good reason for writing for children. But don't forget, if you try to 'preach' too obviously through your writing you will lose sight of your story. And in children's fiction the story *must* remain the most important factor.

James Watson, writer of children's historical fiction, says that when he first started writing he wrote to entertain, to inform and (possibly) educate. He soon discovered, though, that this left out 'the crucial role of being in there; of being it. For a split second, if the illusion has been well-enough staged, the reader is the experience'.

Which brings us to the final, and best, reason for writing for children:

'I want to give them a reading experience they'll never forget.'
Yes! Yes! Yes! Who can forget the first book they ever read? The thrill of watching a child discover a marvellous book for the first time? As the redoubtable Miss Jean Brodie was fond of quoting,

in the film *The Prime of Miss Jean Brodie*: 'Give me a child in her formative years and I'll make her mine for life.'

Bearing this in mind, it is vital therefore that writers for children take their craft seriously and tackle issues in a sensitive and responsible manner. Childhood experiences have a direct link with adult behaviour and so, to a certain extent, the books a child is reading today are shaping the attitudes and society of tomorrow.

THE CHILDREN'S BOOK MARKET AND THE NEW WRITER

The children's book is a rising star in the publishing firmament. Children's literature has been one of the most resilient areas of publishing, tending to withstand economic recessions. Sales in the UK have risen 16% in the past decade – up from £150 million to more than £260 million – and the children's book market is, in fact, now bigger than that for romantic fiction, crime and literary fiction combined.

Schools and libraries have provided a solid source of sales. Figures show that, while library borrowing as a whole continues to decline, children's writing and teenage fiction in particular, shows strong growth. Of the fifty most borrowed authors, sixteen write for the child or teenage market.

UK Public Lending Rights Registrar James Parker has declared that libraries are loth to cut back on children's titles since they support the adult readers and borrowers of the future. Even people who rarely read in their own childhood are now quite likely to buy books for their children. Books are generally seen now as a 'good thing'. The initial novelty impact of satellite/cable television and video and computer games has worn off a little – certainly with parents – and the general feeling is that children should be offered a more stimulating alternative. However, all schools, whether private or state, have limited resources these days and parents cannot necessarily rely on them to provide their children with the best choice of reading material. Even if a child is lucky enough to attend a well financed school, parents are encouraged to back up reading skills taught in school, at home, by taking an interest in books and, where budgets allow, by buying children's books for themselves.

Children's publishing is now starting to attract more media attention as well. Production teams working in television and film are waking up to the fact that just because a piece of fiction is written for children doesn't mean that adults can't enjoy it as well. Books such as *Madam Doubtfire* and *Goggle Eyes* are good, pacey, interesting stories with a wide-ranging appeal, irrespective of the age of the reader. It doesn't surprise me in the least that both attracted huge adult audiences when turned into a film (*Mrs Doubtfire*) and a television series (*Goggle Eyes*). Although based on children's books, films and TV series such as *Mrs Doubtfire* and *Goggle Eyes* have attracted adult audiences and focused adult attention on the children's book world.

The world-renowned book *Sophie's World* by Jostein Gaarder was originally written, and published, as teen fiction, yet it headed the adult bestseller lists in Norway, Germany and the States. The fact is, like many 'children's' books, *Sophie's World* has a wide-ranging appeal and can be enjoyed on a number of different levels. This was quickly recognised by Judith Elliott at Orion who knew that, although adults wouldn't buy a book posing as children's fiction, children *would* buy adult fiction. Another reason for marketing is as an adult book was its length – at over 400 pages it dictated a cover price of £16.99 which took it well outside the normal children's market. All this is good news for the children's writer. A growth in prominence of the children's book market can only mean more openings, and greater opportunities, for those wanting to write for children.

Sifting through the slush pile is extremely labour-intensive. Yet most publishers carry on with this procedure for fear of missing the next bestseller. The list of classic books that have been missed by one publisher and picked up by another is endless and includes *Watership Down* and *Where's Wally* amongst others. I myself have turned down books which have then gone on to be huge successes as published by someone else; I always go and buy a copy to keep on my shelves as a sobering reminder!

Contrary to public opinion, children's publishers are extremely keen to find promising new writers. Hodder Headline sponsor an award (the Fidler Award) set up specifically to encourage previously unpublished, children's writers; the *Independent* also runs a competition, in conjunction with Scholastic, to track down new talent.

But it *is* a very competitive market and writers approaching publishers with material should be aware that their manuscript must display enormous strength and real sales potential to warrant anything other than a polite rejection.

ABOUT THIS BOOK

So how do you learn? How do you make absolutely sure that you are going to get it right? Gone are the days when editors had the time to 'build' authors from scratch. That job has now fallen to the literary agent, but agents won't usually consider representing an author, and spending valuable time working with them, unless they have at least one book under their belt.

In this book I have tried to pass on everything I know about writing for children, picked up from many years in the business as an editor, writer and reader. I have tried to put myself in the place of someone who wakes up one morning and thinks, or, better still, *knows* that 'I want to write a children's book' but doesn't have the first clue where to start.

You *can* do it. But you do have to know what you're doing. This book provides a step by step guide: Part One deals with the market; Part Two with technique; and Part Three with all the practical details that you need to consider once you are ready to approach publishers.

Treat this book rather as you would a correspondence course. Start at the beginning with Lesson One and progress through to the end of the book. Some of the information you will need to know before you can write your first word – some of it you may never need – but it is important to absorb it *all*.

There are exercises at the end of most chapters. Try to do as many as possible. There are many different types of writing for children and the exercises will help you discover which ones are suited to your particular style of creativity.

So imagine. Imagine you are me, sitting at my desk. The phone rings.

'I want to write a children's book,' says the tentative voice on the other end. 'Where do I start?'

Right here. Read on . . .

I

KNOW YOUR MARKET

CHAPTER ONE

THE

PICTURE BOOK

Every book has to start somewhere and I'm starting this one at the youngest end of the children's book market. For those of you who also think that I've started with the easiest option, think again.

> *'There's nothing to those picture books. Money for old rope.'*
> *'There's only a few words on each page. Wouldn't take a second to write.'*
> *'The art's all in the pictures. The writing doesn't matter.'*

These are comments that I have heard made, over the years, about the children's picture book. They are understandable comments but they all fall way short of the truth. The picture book is, in reality, the hardest format to choose if you want to break into the children's market: the hardest to write, and definitely the hardest to sell.

WHAT IS A PICTURE BOOK?

Let's first examine what we actually mean by a 'picture book'; there does seem to be some confusion over the term. Some writers are adamant that they have written a picture book when, in fact, they have written an illustrated children's story. There is a difference.

A picture book is a storybook for the 0–6-year-old age group.

Illustrated in full colour, it has a pre-specified number of pages which is never less than twenty-four and usually not more than forty. It is important to realise that *all* the pages are included in this calculated number, including the front and back covers. The other point to take on board is that the total number of pages must be divisible by eight – twenty-four, thirty-two, forty etc. Generally speaking the twenty-four-page book is for the younger child (0–2 years), the thirty-two-pager for the middle section (3–4 years) and the forty-pager for the older child (5–6 years).

Picture books are rarely more than 1000 words in length and are usually a good deal shorter than this. When Pat Hutchins first wrote *Rosie's Walk*, the text, as she admits, went 'on and on'. After a lot of work she cut it down to just thirty-two words. It works brilliantly.

Rosie's Walk is a book for reading aloud, but there are a number of different styles of picture book. There are early-learning books: alphabet books, nursery rhymes, word books, etc. There are short-story books, books for reading aloud, books for reading alone, books to be looked at, participation books . . . the list goes on!

As a new writer, don't try rhyming texts. These are difficult to translate and, as you read on, you will discover that publishers ideally like to be able to sell the 'rights' of your book abroad.

Novelty books are out as well. These include lift-the-flap books (such as the *Spot* books), bath books, board books, pop-up books, etc. The manufacture of such books is expensive and no publisher will take the financial risk involved with an untried author. These books tend to be specially commissioned or originated in-house.

So why is it such a difficult area?

For a new picture book to be taken on, the publisher first has to be absolutely sure that another country (such as America) will be prepared to publish it as well. This is called a co-edition; by organising co-editions, a publishing house is able to guarantee a much larger initial print run. This, in turn, brings down the unit cost of the book and makes it economically viable. The cost of producing a full-colour book to sell in just one country is, quite frankly, prohibitive.

Selling the idea of a co-edition to foreign publishers often take place at the international book fairs in Frankfurt, London and Bologna. Frankfurt and London deal in general publishing, whereas Bologna is geared up specifically for children's publishing.

Once your picture book has been accepted, in principle, by a British publisher, they may well ask you if they can present your idea at these book fairs. Usually you will be offered some sort of contract to cover this situation and sometimes you will be offered a development fee. It is impossible to be categoric about the amount an author will be offered – it will vary from publisher to publisher. Obviously larger publishers can afford to offer a bigger development fee, with smaller publishers offering much less, if anything at all!

Whether your publisher is able to interest a foreign publisher often depends on the subject matter and the tone of the book. Some genres, particularly humour, work well in one country but do not translate well elsewhere, because of cultural differences. Interest will also depend on whether the foreign publisher feels that the author and illustrator have a proven track record.

At this point I sense that, all over the country, pens and pencils are being hurled across rooms and computers and word processors are being turned off. Pick them up! Turn them back on. Don't despair! It is hard to break into this very competitive sector of the children's market, but it is by no means impossible.

The highly successful children's author, Malorie Blackman, initially found success with her picture book *That New Dress*, which was so good it received offers from two publishers simultaneously. Daniel Postgate broke into the market with his picture book *Kevin Saves the World* and Elizabeth Dale did it with her picture book *Scrumpy*. And those are just three examples that spring immediately to mind.

How do I start?

When writing a picture book you have to first decide whether or not your idea is suited to the picture book style. Is the plot fairly simple? Is there plenty of scope for a wide variety of illustrations?

Winnie the Witch by Korky Paul and Valerie Thomas is an excellent example of a book perfectly suited to its format:

Winnie the Witch lived in a black house. It had black carpets, black chairs, a black bed with black sheets, and black pictures on the walls. It even had a black bath. Winnie lived in her black house with her cat, Wilbur. He was black too. And that is how the trouble began.

The 'trouble' is that Winnie can't see her cat and so she is always falling over him. The book tells the tale of how Winnie changes her black cat first to green, then multi-coloured, and then, when nothing works out, back to black. To get round the problem of not being able to see him, she finally puts a colour spell on her house:

Now instead of a black house, she had a yellow house with a red room and a red door. The chairs were white with red and white cushions. The carpet was green with pink roses. The bed was blue, with pink and white sheets and pink blankets. The bath was a gleaming white.

The plot of this book is intriguingly simple and the text gives plenty of scope for Korky Paul's vibrant illustrations.

This particular book is for the 3–5-year-old and falls to thirty-two pages. However, the author has less than this to work with, as can be seen from the layout chart. Pages one and thirty-two are the front and back outside covers; pages two and thirty-one are the inside covers; page three is blank; page four contains copyright details (ISBN number, publisher's address, publication date, etc), page four is the title page; and page thirty is a blank end page. The story actually starts on page six and ends on page twenty-nine . . . leaving only twenty-four pages for text and illustrations in a thirty-two page book (sixteen in a twenty-four-pager)!

Let's assume that you have an idea which is best suited to a twenty-four page format. Follow a few simple steps in order to construct your story:

1 Write out your text in a straight 'chunk'.
2 Take another piece of paper and list the numbers six to twenty-one down one side. Then work out how your text is

going to divide up on a page-by-page basis and make a note of this by each number.

3   Take a large sheet of paper and map out a layout chart for a twenty-four page book, following the template shown in our illustration. You should end up with twelve halved rectangles.

4   Sketch out, roughly, how you see your layout working. Write in the text on each page showing where it will fall, show where the illustrations will fall (but don't produce illustrations at this stage), where your double-spreads (illustrations and text spread over two adjacent pages) will fall, and so on.

When carrying out this exercise try to make your layout as varied as possible. It does not have to follow the format of a traditional Ladybird book: text on one side and illustration on the other. Some pages could be split into several smaller sections, and some pages may require no text at all.

One good way of ensuring the correct balance of words and pictures is to take a picture book that you feel works well and resembles the type of book you are trying to write, then work backwards, producing a layout chart by following the example of the published book. By analysing the chart it will be clear how the author has structured the book. Copy that same structure for your own work. This is *not* plagiarism. You will (hopefully) end up with a very different story. But until you are more experienced it is an excellent discipline and guide.

Bear in mind the juxtaposition of words and pictures. In many picture books the story is told as much by the pictures as by the words – but it needs an interesting combination of both to work. Children's illustrator, Korky Paul, likens the process to a movie:

'As the drawer you are not only the cinematographer but also the director, the casting agent, the costume designer and responsible for the locations, lighting, props and continuity! The text is the soundtrack and it's that special combination between words and pictures that makes for good storytelling in a picture book. As in a movie, neither can exist properly on their own.'

Take Pat Hutchins' *Rosie's Walk*:

Rosie the hen went for a walk, across the yard, around the pond, over the haycock, past the mill, through the fence, under the beehives, and got back in time for dinner.

On their own, the words are not particularly exciting. Combined with witty and appealing illustrations, however, they become loaded with humour, as we watch the fox unsuccessfully stalking Rosie and having mishap after amusing mishap.

What about the illustrations?

Pat Hutchins is a writer *and* an illustrator. But this is a rare breed indeed! If you honestly feel that you can both write well and illustrate well then by all means have a go. Otherwise I would suggest approaching a publisher with the text only. Make a few suggestions for illustrations but stress that it is the idea and words that you are presenting.

It is not a good idea to approach a publisher with a complete package – in other words with your own text allied to an illustrator's drawings, or vice versa. A publisher might like the text but not the illustrations – or the illustrations but not the text – but will be put off the whole concept because you have presented it as a team effort.

An illustrator is better advised to approach children's design departments direct with a few samples of his/her work. All design departments hold 'banks' of illustrators and are always pleased to discover new, talented illustrators to take onto their books.

If you are that rare writer/illustrator there is no need to spend hours perfecting colour artwork to go with your text. It's better to send a couple of finished colour pages and the rest as roughs. *Never* send original artwork. Colour photocopies might not be a true representation of an artist's work, but they are quite sufficient to enable a publisher to make a judgement.

If you are not an illustrator but nonetheless have very set ideas as to how your book should look, it is perfectly acceptable to say, in your covering letter, something along the lines of: 'I see my book being illustrated in the style of (name illustrator), but I am happy to work with an illustrator of your choice.'

How do I present my work?

In many ways it doesn't matter how you present your work to publishers so long as it is neat and legible. It is also important to make your presentation look as professional as possible. You have to convince the editor that you are not just another amateur wannabe writer: you know what you're doing and it is therefore worth the editor's while to look carefully at your submission.

I would suggesting typing out the text on single-sided white A4 paper, showing the page breaks. For example, the original text submission for *Mummy Laid an Egg!* by Babette Cole would have read:

Page 6: 'Right' said mum and dad. 'We think it's time we told you

Page 7: how babies are made.'

Page 8: 'OK,' we said.

Page 9: 'Girl babies are made from sugar and spice and all things nice,' said mum.

And so on, through to page 34 where the book ends (it is a forty-page picture book – remember these often don't start until page 6).

It's also helpful to present a 'dummy' or a 'mock-up' to go with the straight typed version of the text. A dummy is easily made by taking however many pages you need of A3 paper (A4 can be used, but you don't end up with a lot of space to work with), stacking them together, folding the whole stack in half and then sewing or stapling down the centrefold. For a twenty-four-page book you will need twelve sheets; for a thirty-two-page book sixteen; and so on. The outside sheet (ie. the sheet that forms the front and back cover) can be replaced with coloured paper but this isn't really necessary.

You now have a homemade blank book in which you write the text and brief descriptions (or sketches, if you can draw) of possible illustrations. For example in the dummy of *Mummy Laid an Egg!* Babette would have written the text on page 6 up in the top left-hand corner, with the text on page 7 in the bottom right-hand corner. Write the text in one colour ink and the illustrative description in another, for the sake of clarity. The dummy isn't vital, but it does show the publisher that you can visualise your own work.

What about the writing?

Remember that a child will often want to hear the same picture book read out loud over and over again. This means that your text has to have a rhythm which will leave both the listener and the reader feeling satisfied every time.

Take *That New Dress* by Malorie Blackman and Rhian Nest James. The opening lines have a certain rhythm and that same rhythm is repeated throughout the book:

> Wendy was sad. Wendy was mad. (first page)
> Wendy pouted. Wendy shouted. (page 8)
> Wendy sighed. Wendy cried. (page 10)
> Wendy breathed deep. And had a good weep. (page 12)
> Wendy was glad. And no longer sad. (last page)

It isn't the rhyming that's important, it's the way the words sound:

> He dug his spade into the soil; in, out, in out – and he smiled. (page 9)
> And he threw his ball against the wall again; up, down, up, down – and Ben smiled. (page 11)

There is a compelling feeling to the words themselves which brings the story alive.

The best picture books are good stories in themselves. But they usually contain a message as well. *Owliver* by Robert Kraus is an enchanting tale of an adventurous baby owl; but it is also a book about self-esteem. Similarly, *Something Else* by Kathryn Cave and Chris Riddell is a poignantly simple tale about . . . well, Something Else. '"You don't belong here," they said. "You're not like us. You're something else."'

The combination of Kathryn Cave's text and Chris Riddell's illustrations brings the character of Something Else alive and teaches the reader that it's OK to be different: 'They were different, but they got along. And when something turned up that really was weird-looking (*a perfectly 'normal' human child!*), they didn't say he wasn't like them and he didn't belong there. They moved right up and made room for him too.

Creators of children's television characters often approach editors thinking that their ideas will translate into saleable picture books. This is seldom the case. TV cartoon characters appeal in a very immediate, superficial way; a good picture book will, hopefully, have more depth and be remembered.

Picture Book Exercise

- Think of your own original idea for a picture book.
- Write out the text without worrying about pagination.
- Find a published picture book that you feel works well.
- Create a layout chart for it, noting how the story and pictures are structured.
- Using your own idea and text, copy the layout, trying to keep to approximately the same number of words.
- Make up a dummy and try out your book on a young child. (To maintain their interest it is sometimes a nice idea to ask them to 'fill in' the pictures.)

CHAPTER TWO

READING SERIES

'A serious read?' queried one of my authors, mishearing me as I described the next stage up from the picture book. I had, in fact, said the *Series* Read but, in many ways, the author was right. Reading *Series* are a more *serious* read than picture books – not in quality, but in quantity.

WHAT ARE READING SERIES?

Don't let the term 'Reading Series' fool you. This is not, as the name suggests and many potential authors believe, the publisher's way of extracting a series of books from one particular writer. Indeed, nothing puts off an editor more than a new, untried writer claiming they are working on 'a series' before they have had even one book accepted!

The Series Read is, in fact, a book aimed at children who are just learning to read. Usually they are illustrated with black and white line drawings or, at the younger end of the market sometimes full or part colour.

Publishers group titles together, under a series name, and target them at certain age levels. There will, of course, be some overlap in age range with the picture book market, but publishers see the age range for reading series as being from around 5–6 years, up to around 8–9 years. Each different series will conform to an easily identifiable look and length, and will have a consistent level of language and vocabulary, even though they might be by different authors. The idea is that if children find a book they like, they will want to go on to read other titles in the same series, and these titles will be immediately identifiable on the bookshelves.

The Reading Series market is a huge one – and certainly one of the most receptive as far as a new author is concerned. There are two reasons for this. Firstly, the market is so huge – often the largest area on any publisher's list – that there is plenty of scope for new material. Most series are ongoing and publishers need to publish a certain number of new titles every year to fulfil the requirements of each series.

Secondly, the series read book is marketed using the title of a particular series, as opposed to the name of an author. This makes it easier – and less risky financially as far as the publisher is concerned – to promote new authors, as once a series is established it will go on selling no matter who writes for it.

For the purposes of this book I have decided to split this vast market into two distinct sections – Series Readers and Series Fiction.

Series Readers

You will hear this section of the Series Read market called a number of different things: Series Readers; Picture Storybooks; First Storybooks; Reading Series; and so on. It's confusing, but don't worry – it all boils down to the same thing in the end.

All mainstream publishers produce Series Readers of one kind or another. Rather like the Three Bears, some produce big ones, some produce medium-sized ones and some produce small ones. Knowing who, exactly, produces what is usually the most bewildering aspect of this market for the new author.

Tips on researching the market are dealt with in detail later in this book, but many of the different series are listed in *The Writers' & Artists' Yearbook* in their section on 'Writing and Illustrating Children's Books'. This book has the advantage of being updated every year so the information is as current and accurate as possible.

There are three basic Series Reader categories: Young Readers, Middle Readers and Older Readers.

Young Readers are very short books (hardly longer than a

picture book) for the child of 4–7 years. The length varies but is generally between 1000 and 3000 words. Cartwheels (Hamish Hamilton), Blue Bananas (Heinemann) and Beginners (Orchard Books) are all between 1000 and 1500 words; Jets (A&C Black), Yellow Bananas (Heinemann), Story Books (Macdonald), Read Alones (Orchard Books), Gazelles (Hamish Hamilton) and Corgi Pups (Transworld) are 2000–3000.

Middle Readers are a little longer and more substantial than Young Readers and are targeted at the 6–9 year age range. Length is usually from 3000–7000 words. Sprinters (Walker Books) and Tigers (Anderson) are between 3000–4000; Jumbo Jets and Chillers (A&C Black) are between 4000–5000; whereas Antelopes (Hamish Hamilton) and Kites (Viking) are around 7000 words.

Older Readers are more like short novels, because of the age range they are aimed at and the subject matter they are dealing with. They are usually targeted at the 9–12 year age range and can vary in length from as little as 7000 words to as much as 12,000 words. Red Bananas (Heinemann) are 7000 words, Story Books (Hodder Headline) are 8000–12,000 words and Surfers (Hamish Hamilton) are around 12,000 words.

There are a few Readers around which extend to even more than 12,000 words – Scholastic's Hippo series is one example of this. However, these Readers really cross over into the Stand Alone market which we will be covering in the next chapter. If you want to give your story the best possible chance of publication as a Series Reader you will be sensible to keep it well within the 12,000-word upper limit.

With the exception of the very youngest Readers (such as Cartwheels, which consist of continuous, uninterrupted text) most of these books are divided into chapters; the shorter the total word length, the shorter the chapters.

To make them more attractive for the young child they can be illustrated with a mixture of colour illustrations and black and white line drawings. Sometimes they are illustrated in full colour throughout.

Now, if you are getting all hot and bothered at the very mention of illustrations because you can't even draw pin-people, calm down and take a deep breath. Illustrations for the Series

Reader market are there only to add interest to the text and to make the book seem more accessible for the child. Unlike when writing a picture book, the author does *not* have to consider illustrations when coming up with an idea. Publishers will happily match an illustrator with your text, should it be accepted.

Some Series Readers (Jets and Chillers are two examples) are exceptions to this rule. These have a closely integrated plot and sub-plot; the sub-plot takes place through the illustrations. For example, in *Monty, The Dog Who Wears Glasses* by Colin West (Jets), Monty follows his two young owners to, then into, school. Once inside the school the text reads: 'Monty took the first corridor.' The illustration, however, shows Monty innocently walking into the Staff Room thinking: 'Perhaps they're in here.' The humour and the story are enhanced by the juxtaposition of main text, pictures and sub-text.

It is therefore worth thinking about your story and whether or not it offers scope for a sub-text – if it does it might be right for this particular market.

Do consider which Reader series your story is best suited to. Each Reader series has a slightly different 'feel' and the only way to get to grips with the differences between them is by reading as many as possible. To give you some idea of how varied Series Readers can be, here is a summary of the storyline of four titles.

The Romantic Giant by Kaye Umansky (Cartwheel) tells of Waldo, the giant, who is in love with Princess Clarissa. His next-door neighbour, Heavy Hetty (who, incidentally, is a wrestler and fancies Waldo something rotten!) tries to convince Waldo that Clarissa won't be interested in him. But Waldo is determined to marry Clarissa and tries out a string of romantic ideas to attract her attention.

Don't Let It Rain by Yvonne Coppard (a Piccadilly Pip) is the story of Ben, a little boy who can't wait for his birthday party in the park. But horrible Belinda wants it to rain and Ben knows that she *always* gets her own way. Ben has to do something – has to stop his party from being ruined.

The Unknown Planet by Jean Ure is about Finn and his sister, Shimma, who, with fifty other children, are on board a spaceship searching for a new world. Their own planet, Aqua, is dying and can no longer support them. Suddenly the alarm rings – their spaceship, *Sea Queen*, is about to make a crash landing on an unknown planet.

The Stray Cat's Tale by Ian Strachan tells of Milda, the kitten, who strays from her mother when chasing a feather across a field. This is the story of Milda's eventful journey to a new home.

As you can see from just four examples, Series Readers can have storylines ranging from the modern fairytale, to everyday events, to science fiction, to animal adventure. It doesn't really matter what you decide to write about – so long as the style and content suits the Reader series you are targeting.

Vocabulary must be simple, clear and unsophisticated. Plots must be action-based and uncluttered and writing style should be pacey and direct. The one thing to bear in mind when writing for any Series Reader (Chillers included) is that humour, whether zany or more gentle, is a key element for this age group.

Writing the Reader: Exercises

- Pay a visit to the children's section of your local library or bookshop and study some of the Series Readers mentioned in this chapter.
- Think of your own idea for a Series Reader.
- Based on what you have read, try to establish what age group your idea is for and how long (in words) it will be.
- With a particular Reader series in mind, plot out your book chapter by chapter, remembering to take into account the number of words in each chapter (for example, a 3000-word Yellow Banana of five chapters will have only 600 words in each chapter).

Series Fiction

When I talk about Series Fiction I mean literally that – a series of fiction books with the same generic title. They can be written by one author, by lots of authors or, alternatively, by a number of different authors writing under a single pseudonym. The highly successful *Animal Ark* series, published by HodderHeadline, written by Lucy Daniels, is a good example of Series Fiction. Even more well known is the *Goosebumps* series by R.L. Stine, published by Scholastic.

Although Series Fiction titles are published by the same publishers who produce Readers, they are usually commissioned in a different way. This is because they often come from packagers.

What on earth are 'packagers', I hear you ask? You'll hear more about them when I talk about non-fiction later in the book. However, as far as Series Fiction is concerned a packager is a company which comes up with the idea for a particular series and then persuades a publisher to take it on.

It works along the following lines: Bill and Ben of Flowerpot Men International (a UK packager) have just finished doing a presentation to the Editorial Director of Gosling Books (a big children's publisher). They have demonstrated to the Editorial Director that there is a gap in the pony books market for girls of around 8–10 years. They have suggested, to fill this gap, a series of short books about a family who run a riding stables in a London suburb. Each book would tell the story of a different adventure set in and around the stables. The heroine of the series would be Pamela the daughter of the family who own the stables.

'Great stuff!' says the Editorial Director. 'We'll do it.' (Of course real life isn't usually like that. In real life the Editorial Director would probably say, 'I'll get back to you next week,' and six months later Bill and Ben would be none the wiser.)

So Bill and Ben go away and put together a proper brief, which they will send out to agents saying they are looking for writers. The briefs for this type of Series Fiction can vary but they are usually fairly specific. Bill and Ben's would say what sort of girl Pamela is (it could even describe what she looks like), give details of any family and friends they want included in the stories, describe what the riding stables is like (where it is, how big it is, how many ponies, etc) and would go on to outline the plots of the first few books.

Any interested authors would then submit a sample and, if this is satisfactory, will be commissioned to write the entire book. This will be edited by Bill or Ben and presented to the publisher as a complete 'package'.

Many authors are not keen on doing this type of work. Some feel that, because the idea has already been thought through in some detail, it would not be 'their' work in the true sense of the word. Other authors find the discipline of working to someone else's brief too demanding. Some even believe that such a commercial form of fiction is demeaning, and writing under a pseudonym, insulting.

Personally I think that writing Series Fiction is excellent experience for the new writer; it can provide a steady income in an otherwise uncertain market. Top children's agent, Lesley Hadcroft of Laurence Pollinger, calls it 'gas bill money'. However, it is, unfortunately, a fairly inaccessible market as far as the new writer is concerned. How do you, as a new writer, get to hear about new Series Fiction projects? You most likely won't have an agent until you have had a few books published, and editors working on these projects tend to rely on agents for their writers.

There are a number of sensible steps you can take to try and find this kind of work. Firstly, look out for new Series Fiction titles in the shops. If you see a Series developing, check out the publishing (biblio) details on the opening (prelim) pages. Even if you can't work out who the packager is, this page will give you the name of the publisher. Drop them a line, with a sample of writing and details of any relevant experience, asking if they're looking for new authors for that particular Series.

Alternatively, you could always try approaching packagers direct in the same way. There is a list of packagers who deal in children's books in the children's writing section of *The Writers & Artists Yearbook*.

Series Fiction: Exercise

- Pay a visit to the children's section of your local bookshop or library and try to identify as many Series Fiction titles as possible.
- Study the opening pages of each title in the Series carefully and try to work out whether the Series is written by a single author, or by a number of different authors.
- Choose one Series and think of a new idea for another book in the same series, using the same setting and characters.
- Write the first chapter and then do a brief chapter-by-chapter breakdown for the rest of the book.

CHAPTER THREE

READING SCHEMES IN THE EDUCATIONAL MARKET

Reading Schemes? Boring!

That is the attitude of most new writers when confronted with the idea of writing for educational Reading Schemes. Many people have childhood memories of books such as *Janet and John* which had pedestrian or non-existent plots and characterisation that was superficial at best. 'Reading' books in those days (and there are still some hanging on in schools today) existed simply to demonstrate to children developing their reading and writing skills how the English language should be used.

However, you'll be pleased to hear that Reading Schemes have made considerable progress since we were at school and most educational publishers today are producing lively, entertaining books with strong storylines. To achieve this they use 'real' authors (i.e. authors who write for commercial/trade publishers as well) and are always on the lookout for talented new writers to add to their author lists.

WHAT IS A READING SCHEME?

Reading Schemes are books published by educational publishers for specific use in schools. Like Series Readers they conform to an easily identifiable look and length, but as far as writing them is concerned the approach is more akin to Series Fiction, in that the publisher provides the writer with a very detailed brief to work to.

For the author it is a hard market to research because Reading Schemes are usually not sold in bookshops but marketed direct to schools. More often than not Reading Scheme books are only available in 'packs' (with each pack corresponding to a certain reading level) and are not sold as individual titles.

Like Reading Series, the Reading Scheme market is open to new writers because it is the Scheme itself which is being promoted, not the author's name. However, it is a discipline with rigid rules, and this approach doesn't suit everyone.

There is one significant difference between the Series market and the Scheme market: educational publishers will not welcome material based on Schemes that they already publish. The educational market is a fast-moving one and publishers are always looking for new, original Schemes for a whole range of reading.

How to Write a Reading Scheme Book

It's best to make your initial approach to educational publishers by letter. State any relevant experience you may have – they will always be interested to hear from teachers, for example, who have first-hand experience of Reading Schemes – and send a sample of your writing. If your work seems suitable you will be added to their list of authors and sent briefs of any appropriate future schemes.

These briefs can vary enormously. Some take up less than a side of A4, others go on for pages. This is one of the more simple variety, from Ginn:

Reading 360 Pocket Books Levels 6, 7 and 8, Third Set
The Pocket Book series is a popular and successful range of illustrated paperbacks for newly independent readers. The books are grouped in Levels, which correspond to Levels 6 and 12 of Ginn's Reading 360 Scheme. These books are intended to be used as supplements to the main 360 Scheme and authors do not, therefore, have to worry about using a restricted vocabulary.

There are already eight books at each Level, and next year we are hoping to bring out a further set of four books at each of Levels 6, 7 and 8. Books in Level 6 are, on average, between 1500 and 2000 words long, and Level 8 books are usually between 2300 and 2500 words long.

Level 6 books are intended to appeal to children aged about six, and should be fairly simple in terms of plot and language level. Levels 7 and 8 are aimed at seven and eight-year-olds, and can be slightly more complex, although simple, easily readable language and good, exciting plots are essential. We are looking for stories on a wide range of subjects, including family and friends, school, adventure, animals, dinosaurs, magic (though probably not ghosts or witches), sports, confronting fears, and fantasy. Stories with a multicultural background are particularly welcome.

You will note that this particular brief stresses that there is to be no use of 'controlled vocabulary'. However, a structured use of vocabulary is very important in many Reading Schemes, with specified words being carefully added to each level, building gradually on vocabulary used in the previous level.

The following extract is adapted from a Heinemann author brief for their Storyworlds Reading Scheme (Stage 8) and shows just how demanding restricted vocabulary writing can be. Heinemann gave their authors a list of 70 new words to be intro-duced into the Stage 8 books (see list) and then set out the fol-lowing requirements:

We are aiming to produce enjoyable stories which enable the child to read with confidence and so we ask authors to draw on a set list of words which gradually increases from stage to stage. These words should be repeated within a story to reinforce children's understanding of them. How-ever, repetition should be as natural and subtle as possible.

In addition to the words on the list, please feel free to use simple, well-known nouns, but where possible these should be nouns that can be cued from the pictures. Please also try to think about the ways in which words are 'sounded out' phonically when choosing words (eg. 'jug' is easier to read than 'vase'). The ending 's' can be used to create plural nouns but more complex plurals should be avoided.

All two-letter words can be used even if they do not

WRITING BOOKS FOR CHILDREN

appear on the word list. Simple three-letter words can be used as well. The language of the stories should be a mixture of present tense, direct speech and past tense narrative. All sentences should be as direct as possible.

All verbs on the list can also be used with the 'ed', 's' and 'ing' endings. At this stage we can now introduce the use of more complex verb changes (eg. swim/swam, or throw/threw). Authors should still try to avoid more difficult changes, such as think/thought, unless they are on the word list.

The adverbial ending 'ly' can now be added to words on the list (eg. 'slowly' can be used as well as 'slow').

Apostrophes can be used to show possession and also to form contractions of any of the words on the list.

Any words that can be formed from other words on the list can be used (eg. to + day, some + where).

always	anything	argue	awake	behind
best	better	carry	chase	click
clumsy	deep	dream	even	ever/y
fair	follow	full	happen	hard
heavy	hope	hungry	kind	know
last	long	lost	loud	mind
miss	morning	need	never	nice
noise	poor	quiet	rain	real
rich	self	sent	shot	should
shout	side	slept	slow	small
smell	smile	sneeze	stay	stick
stupid	suddenly	through	time	tired
told	trust	turn	understand	until
warm	wave	while	wise	work
write				

The brief also instructed that stories should have a strong sense of adventure, have a clear beginning, middle and end, that plots should move forwards and not 'zig-zag', that the stories should be aimed at ages 6–7 and appeal equally to boys and girls. It went on to specify various subject categories – *Our World*, *Animal World*, *Fantasy World*, *Once-Upon-a-Time World* and so on.

The 'no zig-zagging' instruction is important when writing for the Reading Scheme market. This type of 'learning to read' story must be very direct in approach and the plots should move forward without referring to past or future events. This is because the primary objective in the Reading Scheme book is to educate children in reading techniques. One senior editor describes it as 'reading the lines, as opposed to reading *between* the lines'. In other words, there is no room for inferred meaning. The plots and writing style have to be clear and straightforward, and all Reading Scheme stories must have a well defined and simple structure.

Sounds simple, doesn't it? Well, it isn't! The briefs have such detailed requirements that they can seem extremely complicated and they must be studied very carefully.

One of the most complicated author briefs I have ever come across was for the Ginn Supersonics Reading Scheme. This consisted of four extensive phonic word lists, including three-letter words with short vowels (jet, let, net, etc), four- and five-letter words beginning with a blend or digraph (flat, slat, chat, etc), single-syllable words with short vowel sounds which end in L, F, S, K (ball, cuff, kiss, deck, etc), single-syllable words with short vowels and common letter strings (bang, fang, gang, etc), and both simple and more complex two-syllable words and four- and five-letter words using the 'magic e' (cake, make, rake, etc).

The brief then read as follows:

Style of Text
The stories can be in the following styles:
● rhyming couplets
● four- to six-line verses with a regular rhyme scheme
● text which does not rhyme in the same way as verse but which uses internal rhyme, repetition of sounds within a sentence and/or recurring refrains.

Amount of Text per Page
Please try to have one 'unit of sense' on each page – in other words, one whole couplet, a short verse or a paragraph. Don't worry too much about the total number of words per page, but try to keep it to the equivalent of up to four short sentences.

Using the Word Lists

Look at the word lists for all four sets. Choose one or two vowel sounds from Set 4, and then some of the patterns from Set 3 to go with these. To make sensible sentences out of these words, use words from List 1 and any other words you feel you need. Don't be afraid to use two-syllable words at this stage, either by adding suffixes like 'ed' and 'ing' or by combining two single-syllable words . . .

It is important to focus on just one or, at the most, two of the long vowel sounds in Set 4 (preferably not the long o). It should be clear from the text which patterns you have chosen, but you can take liberties with the words and use odd combinations – the idea is to have fun, and to make it fun for the reader too!

It all sounds rather off-putting. But don't be dissuaded. One of Ginn's authors is Jill Atkins, who came up with *Jake the Snake* for this set. Believe it or not, Jill says that it *was* fun to write, as well as being a real challenge. All it requires is a bit of concentration and discipline.

> At the side of a big fishing lake,
> There lived an old viper called Jake
> He got his fang stuck
> In a deep pile of muck
> He was really a silly old snake!

The educational market is a hard one to satisfy. Once publishers have put together the framework of a Reading Scheme, it is 'trialed' in schools across the country, and there are no sterner critics than children themselves. For this reason any writer wanting to contribute to this demanding genre should be aware of current teaching methods in primary schools. If you are not in day-to-day contact with young children (or even if you are), offer your services to your local primary school. Most primary schools have too many pupils and too few teachers, and will be only too happy to receive offers of voluntary help. As a writer you can either read your work to selected classes, or, more usefully, hear children read. When a teacher has a class of thirty or more children of very mixed ability it is a godsend when someone is prepared to take a few of those children out of the classroom to give them individual help. It goes without saying, though, that if you are not known to the primary school concerned you should first make a formal approach to the Head Teacher in writing, stating exactly what you are offering and why.

Once you are working within the school system you will soon realise (unless you live in a very remote rural area) that the children in each class are from a wide variety of social and ethnic backgrounds. For this reason Reading Scheme texts are scrutinised intensely for political correctness. If you want to write for this market, you should be aware of this scrutiny and bear with it. For example, pigs may be loveable creatures – but Reading Schemes are destined for distribution throughout the entire country, including areas where large Moslem communities reside. Pigs are, for Moslems, taboo, and should therefore be avoided in Reading Scheme plots. Otherwise publishers not only risk causing major offence but may also alienate themselves from a large sector of the buying market.

When Reading Schemes are trialed in schools children are quick to pick out oddities of language or plot; but they are equally quick to say what they enjoy. The Senior Commissioning Editor for Cambridge Reading tells of a rewarding moment when she was reading a dummy of *Seal* with a group of children, one of whom was very shy. The children enjoyed the book and they discussed it with the editor in some detail. When the bell went for playtime, the shy child didn't want to go. 'Oh no,' she said, 'I want to read it again.'

After reading the book several more times she said, very excitedly, 'I'm going to go home and tell Mummy that I read a whole book!'

Reading Scheme: Exercise

Write a short story for children who are just beginning to read (5–6 year olds) using the restricted word list below.

Points to remember:
1 Stories should be between 300–400 words.
2 Stories should be simple, with a beginning, a middle and an end. Choose a subject that children of this age and experience

will be interested in: starting school, dragons, animals, teddy bears, family life, dinosaurs.

3 Set the story out on sixteen pages with Page 1 as the title page. Try to divide up the words fairly equally between pages.

4 Keep sentences short and avoid sub-clauses. Each sentence should be no more than eight or nine words long, and there should be no more than six lines of text per page.

5 Do not use indirect speech; *John said he would go.* Instead use direct speech: *'I will go,' said John.*

6 You may add to the word list by using characters' names (keep them simple) and any proper nouns that can be illustrated with a picture, so that if the reader does not know the word, he or she will be able to guess it from the illustration.

a	can't	gave	home	make
over	take	was	all	come
get	I	me	play	thank
we	am	could	give	if
must	put	that	went	an
cross	go	in	my	ran
the	were	and	day	going
into	no	run	them	what
as	did	good	is	not
sad	then	when	are	do
got	it	now	said	there
where	ask	don't	had	jumped
off	saw	they	who	at
down	happy	just	of	see
this	why	big	eat	have
laugh	old	she	to	will
blew	fell	he	laughed	on
sleep	too	wish	but	find
help	let's	one	so	tried
with	by	flew	her	little
open	some	under	would	called
fly	here	like	or	something
up	yes	came	for	him
looked	our	stop	very	you
can	from	his	made	out
swim	want	your		

CHAPTER FOUR

STAND-ALONE FICTION FOR 8–12 YEAR OLDS

The mechanics of reading have (hopefully) been mastered by the time a child is eight; they can then venture into the big, wide world of independent reading. However, note that I have called this chapter *Stand-Alone Fiction For 8–12 Year Olds* and not *Stand-Alone Fiction*. This is because, technically, the term Stand-Alone Fiction includes any book which isn't published as either a Picture Book or as part of a Reading Series.

So *The Last Polar Bears* by Harry Horse, *Tingleberries, Tuckertubs and Telephones* by Margaret Mahy (Hamish Hamilton) and *The Little Wolf's Book of Badness* by Ian Whybrow are all Stand-Alone Fiction. These titles quite literally 'stand alone', with no identification on the cover and spine except the book title, the author name, the illustrator name (if there are illustrations) and the publishing 'imprint' (more about imprints later). They are all fairly short, illustrated and targeted at readers under the age of eight.

However, if you submit a book in a similar style to a children's publisher, expect the following responses:

'What are we supposed to do with it?'
'It's neither one thing, nor the other. Too long/not right for Picture Books/Series Fiction, too short/not right for Stand-Alone Fiction'.
'Who is this book for? It doesn't fall into any specific category.'

But if that's the case, I hear you thinking, how come Harry Horse/Margaret Mahy/Ian Whybrow got their Stand-Alone Fiction published?

As far as Margaret Mahy and Ian Whybrow are concerned, the answer is that they are well-known children's authors with proven track records, writing material of such exceptional quality that no editor in their right mind would turn their books down. In Harry Horse's case the answer is luck (plus a large dollop of talent!).

But *you* don't have a proven track record and you can't rely on luck. So you have to give yourself the *best possible* chance of publication. Of course you can write a book of any old length, about any old subject, and submit it to any old publisher – and of course they may pounce on it with wild enthusiasm and proclaim it to be the best thing since *Winnie the Pooh*. However, the likelihood is that this won't happen. The likelihood is that your typescript will wing its way back to you with thanks, but 'no thanks' stamped all over it.

Even Harry Horse only made it by the skin of his teeth. *The Last Polar Bears* is a collection of fictional letters from a grandfather to his grandchild, written while the grandfather was on an expedition to the North Pole to find – yes, you guessed it – the last polar bears. Harry designed his submission to look as if the letters had been parcelled up and sent direct from the North Pole; they were written on carefully antiquated parchment paper, bundled up in crinkly brown paper (complete with picturesque date stamps from all over the world) and tied up with string. As a result several publishers mistook the package as being from a dotty old lady and didn't even bother to open it.

The point I'm making is this: it is the *minority* of published Stand-Alone books which are shorter and targeted at the younger reader and, as we saw above, usually these are by authors already known to the publisher. For the most part Stand-Alone Fiction is longer, more complex and for the older market.

How Long?

Too long, in my opinion, is anything over 40,000 words. Too short is anything under 15,000 words. Everything in between is fine.

The 40,000 word novel is, of necessity, going to need a higher cover price – which, in turn, will make it harder to sell. The novel of less than 15,000 words is better targeted at the Reading Series market.

So what does 15,000/20,000/40,000 words actually look like? Let's take a few well-known titles. *Watership Down* by Richard Adams and *Goodnight Mister Tom* by Michelle Magorian are both well over 40,000 words; *Bill's New Frock* by Anne Fine is around 15,000 words; *The Sheep-Pig* by Dick King-Smith and *Matilda* by Roald Dahl are around 20,000 words.

You can argue this question of a 'right' length until the cows come home. And, believe me, some authors do!

'But my book's as long as it's long.'
'My text dictates its length to me, not the other way round.'
'But I couldn't possibly cut it. It's all far too good!'

These are some of the comments levelled at me as an editor when I dare to suggest that a submission is being turned down purely on grounds of its length.

You can't argue with the facts. It's not going to do much for a child's 'street cred' if, at the age of eight-plus when they have enough reading confidence to choose a more ambitious book outside of the Reading Series market, he or she can only find thin, unimpressive-looking 'baby' books. On the other hand, Oxford University Press say that Pat O'Shea's novel *The Hounds of the Morrigan* (some 400 pages or so) was turned down by ten publishers before eventually finding a home with them. Ten rejection letters – most writers would have long since given up!

When renowned children's author, Kathleen Fidler, died shortly after her eightieth birthday, many people felt that her tireless support for children's reading should not go unrecognised. In 1982 the Kathleen Fidler Award was launched to encourage new writing for children between the ages of eight and twelve (more about this in Part III). It is interesting to note that submissions should be between 20–25,000 words in length to satisfy the rules of the award.

My vote goes to Kathleen Fidler. If you are writing for this age group, 20–25,000 words is a sensible length to aim for.

Subject Matter

The fun part about writing for 8–12-year olds is that you can write about almost anything. The serious, the funny, the outrageous and the downright controversial will all be considered if centred around a strong, original and relevant theme.

We'll explore themes in detail in Part II of this book but, for the purposes of this chapter, I'll briefly run through the various types of Stand-Alone books you may consider writing.

Historical Fiction

Any story set entirely in the past (and this can be anything up to, and including, the advent of the Beatles!) can be described as historical fiction.

Examples: *Goodnight Mister Tom* by Michelle Magorian and *Andi's War* by Billi Rosen.

Time-Slip Stories

These are stories which move backwards or forwards (and sometimes both) through time. Often a plot set in the present will run parallel with a plot from the past or future, with some linking factor.

Examples: *The Naming of William Rutherford* by Linda Kempton and *James Bodger and the Priory Ghost* by Gene Kemp.

Fantasy

Fantasy encompasses a huge range of subjects but fantasy stories are usually centred around 'other imaginary worlds' inhabited by 'other imaginary creatures'.

Examples: *The Dark is Rising* by Susan Cooper and *The Howen* by Roger Stevens.

Science Fiction

Terry Pratchett describes Science Fiction as 'Fantasy with bolts on'. Indeed, as far as children's books are concerned, Fantasy and Science Fiction can often be merged together to produce a separate category, Science Fantasy. Pure Science Fiction is perhaps more 'logical' than fantasy and encompasses futuristic stories set on Earth, other planets and other hemispheres. The sky is, quite literally, the limit.

Examples: *Children of the Dust* by Louise Lawrence and *A Tale of Time City* by Diana Wynne Jones.

Fairy Tales

Fairy Tales for this age group are more akin to Fantasy than to the traditional tales of Princes and Princesses aimed at a younger age group. The authors borrow imagery and happenings from the Fairy Tale powerhouse and their stories include an element of enchantment intertwined with the main story.

Examples: *The Other Side of Silence* by Margaret Mahy and *Castle Gryffe* by Eileen Dunlop.

Adventure Stories

This will be a plot-driven, action-based book, but writers should be aware that without strong characterisation the story will be considered too one-dimensional.

Examples: *Hacker* by Malorie Blackman and *Run, Zan Run* by Catherine MacPhail.

Horror and Ghost Books

Because a Horror or Ghost Book must be horrific or scary in some way, these are usually for the older end of the 8–12 age range. Like adventure stories they are plot-driven and action-based, but also have an element of the horrific or supernatural.

Examples: *Gilray's Ghost* by John Gordon (very much for the upper end) and *The Watch House* by Robert Westall.

Funny Books

By Funny Books I do not mean some other category of book which also happens to be funny, but books where the author has actually set out to be humorous from start to finish.

Examples: *How I Became a Star and Other Homework Excuses* by Jon Blake and *The Secret Diary of Adrian Mole aged 13¾* by Sue Townsend.

People Books

This last category covers books which can't really be described as adventure stories in the true sense of the word, but don't fit into any other category either; although they do have compelling plots, they are essentially centred round the characters contained within the plot framework.

Examples: *Krindlekrax* by Philip Ridley and *Master of Secrets* by Ruth Symes.

WRITING STAND-ALONE FICTION

Of course, it is often impossible to categorise books quite so neatly. Philip Ridley's *Krindlekrax* is a People Book – but it is also an Adventure Story and a Funny Book, with a little bit of Fantasy and Fairy Tale thrown in for good measure. *The Howen* is Fantasy, but it is also an Adventure Story with some Horror included.

Too many writers producing material for this age group think that their best chance of publishing success is to emulate the bestsellers: that they either have to write an Adventure Story in the style of Enid Blyton, or a Funny Book in the style of Roald Dahl. Both writers wrote wonderful and extremely popular books – but they are unique, and any imitation is a waste of time. *Be original*. Not only because imitations are easy to spot, but because children's publishing is very innovative and creative and new ideas will find more favour than recycled old ones. When doing your reading research, be sure to read books by contemporary living authors as well as dead ones! Observe children you know in this age group – what do they like to read? What are their interests and hobbies?

When coming up with ideas for the 8–12 age group it is important to keep your mind as open as possible. Never rule anything out on the grounds that it isn't 'suitable' or is 'too old'. Children in this age range are just starting to realise that life isn't as simple as they once thought and they are perfectly capable of handling 'grown-up' subjects so long as they are presented in an accessible way.

Take the following passage from *Goodnight Mister Tom* by Michelle Magorian:

The small alcove stank of stale urine and vomit. A thin emaciated boy with matted hair and skin like parchment was tied to a length of copper piping. He held a small bundle in his arms. His scrawny limbs were covered with sores and bruises and he sat in his own excrement. He shrank at the light from the torch and made husky gagging noises. The warden reached out and touched him and he let out a frightened whimper. An empty baby's bottle stood by his legs.

The 'bundle' is, in fact, a dead baby. The boy is covered in sores and bruises because he has been violently abused by his own mother and left to die in wartime London during the Blitz. As you can see, this author doesn't shrink from tackling quite disturbing topics – one which would not be out of place in adult fiction.

And how about this harrowing passage from *Chandra* by Frances Mary Hendry:

The old man stared at her, his mouth working under his bushy moustache. 'Roop?' he said, bitterly, 'He died. A week ago. A fever. My son, my youngest son. He's dead.' The women wailed from the darkness. Exhausted and horrified, Chandra knew that they were grieving for Roop's father, not her.

Cursed, struck, and spat upon by everyone, she screamed, begged, wept . . . By the time she was shoved through a doorway and left alone she was half-unconscious. She curled into a ball, crying as quietly as she could. Oh, Roop!

Roop was dead. At eleven years old, she was a widow.

Both these books are aimed at children of nine or ten years upwards, and both deal with subjects which some adults might find shocking. However, they are very much children's books because they tell the story of a nine year-old boy (in the case of *Goodnight Mister Tom*) and an eleven year-old girl (in the case of *Chandra*) entirely from the child's point-of-view. Exclusively adult aspects of these books, such as the boy's mother's suicide in *Goodnight Mister Tom*, or the implications of an under-age marriage in *Chandra*, are dealt with simplistically. The style renders the subject matter palatable, and softens any sharp edges.

Another important factor to consider when writing for this age group – particularly if creating stories based on the more gruelling aspects of life – is that a completely downbeat narrative with no highspots or humour will not be acceptable. Just as editors don't fill their newspapers with only bad news (because no one would buy them!), successful authors don't fill children's books with nothing but negativity.

Ron Heapy, Managing Editor of Oxford University Press Children's Books, puts it succinctly: 'We don't mind if our novels' characters get hurt or suffer in some way. The important thing is that the major players have to change and develop in a *positive* way. At the end of the book there has to be a feeling of hope, a feeling of "Here I am. This is my name."'

I hope I'm not giving too much away if I quote the endings of the two books previously discussed:

Will swallowed a few mouthfuls of tea and put some fresh coke on the range fire. As he observed it tumble and fall between the wood and hot coke, it occurred to him that strength was quite different from toughness, and that being vulnerable wasn't the same as being weak.

He looked up at Tom and leaned forward in his direction.

'Dad,' he ventured.

'Yes,' answered Tom, putting down his library book. 'What is it?'

'Dad,' repeated Will, in a surprised tone, 'I'm growing.'

(Goodnight Mister Tom)

For a moment Chandra quailed. It was tempting the gods to say such a thing! She'd like to believe it, but . . .

Her heart swelled. She hugged Aunt Manju back, with a suddenly joyful strength. She was alive, and free, with a new family and a new life in front of her. She'd make more friends. The world did change. She would believe it. Even if all her troubles weren't over, she'd manage.

She was Chandra!

(Chandra)

See? Not a dry eye in the house, but you still feel like dancing down the aisles!

Philip Ridley is probably one of the most popular writers for this age group so I'll let him have the final say:

'I'm increasingly concerned to help children confront their problems. My stories are obsessed with all the modern sources of anxiety: with money, poverty, vanity, ageing, decay, but I want to express these anxieties in a way that cuts through all that stuff to the core of what really matters, which is, I suppose, a kind of solidarity in adversity. In *Krindlekrax* it's Ruskin's love for his friend the school-keeper that causes him to confront the dragon, and in doing so to heal a whole street. *Meteorite Spoon* is almost entirely about violent argument and disappointment, but in the end the children teach their parents the value of love. If I had to sum up what I'm trying to do in my books, I'd say it's an attempt to make children feel less lonely in their fears.'

Stand-Alone Fiction: Exercises

- Consider the different subject matters listed in this chapter and establish which area you think you might be most qualified to write about.
- Pay a visit to your local children's library or bookshop and browse through as many titles (contemporary authors, as well please!) as possible which handle your chosen subject matter.
- Think of your own idea for a Stand-Alone Fiction title.
- Write a one-page story outline, based on your idea (but do not plot it out in detail until you have read the chapters on 'Theme' and 'Plotting' in Part II).

Chapter five

Teenage Fiction

Publishers' trade magazine the *Bookseller* asked its readers recently, when is a teenage book not a teenage book? Answer, when it looks like being so successful that adult lists want it too.

This is what happened to *Sophie's World* by Jostein Gaarder, which was 'discovered' in this country by Judith Elliott of Orion Children's Books. Despite this, and despite also the fact that *Sophie's World* was originally published in Norway as a teenage novel, the book was eventually published in the UK by Phoenix House, an adult imprint of Orion Books. Elliott, told the *Bookseller*. 'We are publishing it as an adult book because *we felt it could reach a wider audience*'.

Which pretty well sums up the problems involved in trying to create a book specifically targeted at teenagers. Teenagers – *real* teenagers – (i.e. children of thirteen-plus) don't read Teenage Fiction, they read Adult Books. This makes the term teenager a bit of a misnomer. Some publishers/librarians/booksellers have tried to circumnavigate this problem by re-naming this publishing category Young Adult Fiction. Nonetheless, despite this attempt to give Teenage Fiction wider appeal, all children's publishers recognise that teenage books are in fact read and enjoyed by children as young as ten.

If you don't believe me go and spend some time in your local children's library during term-time. Third- and Fourth-Year Juniors will pounce on the teenage shelves with enthusiasm. However, children at Secondary level won't be seen dead in the children's section. These older children are more likely to be in the adult library, acting cool, plucking reading material from under the noses of more senior readers.

There is one argument which suggests that there should be no formal separation between teenage reading and adult reading: that books specifically targeted at the teenager are a fairly recent phenomenon imported from America. Indeed, children's author, Adèle Geras, believes that writers should forget about their audience altogether, and write entirely to please themselves. She says: 'The less-than-good teenage books happen, I think, when a writer sits down and says to herself, "I'm going to write a book that'll go down a bomb with all the groovy dudes down at the disco." That's writing a book *de haut en bas*, and it shows. Always.'

However (as all you aspiring teenage writers will be glad to hear!) there is a market for Teenage Fiction, albeit fairly small. Teenage Fiction is aimed at children in the age range of approximately 11–16 – a very wide band. These years can be fraught with turbulent emotion and insecurities and Teenage Fiction can help young people explore often very disturbing feelings in a safe and unembarrassing way. It is performing a social function: acting as a reassuring, sympathetic and wise best friend.

SUBJECT MATTER

Critics often complain that Teenage Fiction is too issue-based; and certainly many titles in this genre do deal with subjects like sexuality, death, war, broken families, etc. However, teenagers themselves like nothing more than reading about the experiences of their own age group and, at this age, are able to internalise their emotional reactions to texts. For example, Malorie Blackman's short story 'Child's Play' (from her collection of teenage short stories *Not So Stupid!*) has been used in schools to spark off discussion about prejudice – particularly racial prejudice – but also general prejudice against those we feel to be different from ourselves in some way:

'I know this is going to be hard to believe but it's true. Susaine isn't like us. She's not . . . well, she's not from this planet . . .'

'Well I could've told you that,' 'I frowned. 'Come on, Janet, get to it!'

'I'm serious. Susaine's from another planet.'

I sat back, disappointed. 'Don't talk wet,' I said, scathingly. And here I'd been looking forward to a juicy secret.

'I'm serious,' Janet replied angrily. 'And what's more, I can prove it.'

'Go on then,' Elli challenged, as disappointed as I was.

'She doesn't have any blood.'

Silence.

'WHAAT?!' I asked, not sure that I had heard correctly.

'She doesn't have any blood,' Janet repeated triumphantly.

Needless to say, Susaine *does* have blood – but unfortunately the girls only finally prove this after stabbing her to death. The story therefore makes a serious point in a way to which teenagers can relate.

In the most recent edition of teenage magazine *Our Choice* – described as a list of 'good reads' recommended by teenagers for teenagers – the Young Book Trust, who produces the publication, splits Teenage Fiction into twelve different categories: Real-Life Stories; Families; Humour; Romance; The Past; Future Worlds; Science Fiction; Fantasy; Horror; Mysteries; The Supernatural; Thrillers. As with Stand-Alone Fiction, the lines are blurred between some of these categories – a mystery novel may contain elements of the supernatural, for example, and a Real-Life Story may be centred around the Family. But it's interesting that the teenagers themselves seem to have a very clear idea about which category novels fit into. Their 'reviews' give you a much more precise flavour of what Teenage Fiction is all about – and the nature of its appeal – than any adult critique.

Real-Life Stories:
Flour Babies by Anne Fine

Class 4C have to do 'child development' for the annual school science fair and Simon Martin finds himself looking after a Flour Baby (a six-pound bag of flour). It puts his parental skills to the test and makes him think about his father, who left when he was a few weeks old.

Simon Martin was mostly a 'stupid kid' but his true, caring feelings emerge when he talks to his Flour Baby. I enjoyed this book a lot. It is both funny and sad. I could read it again and again.

Gemma Connolly (14), Saint Benedict School

Families
Do-Over by Rachel Vail

I enjoyed this book immensely because it is written from a teenager's point of view. It is about a boy who finds life complicated, particularly in dealing with his parents' separation and coping with relationships with girls. I could really identify with what he was going through.

Bonnie McLellan (13), Great Conard Upper School

Humour
The Boyfriend Trap by Mary Hooper

Teri goes to stay with her older sister, Sarah. She decides that Sarah needs a boyfriend, but trying to find one for her leads Terri into all kinds of comic mishaps with a number of unsuitable candidates.

A really good book, one of the best and funniest that I have ever read. Very highly recommended.

Caroline Goddard (13), Soham Village College

Romance
I Never Loved Your Mind by Paul Zindel

This contemporary American story is told from the viewpoint of 17-year-old Dewey Daniels. Although he is incredibly intelligent, he drops out of High School and takes a job in a hospital where he meets Yvette Goethals. At first she doesn't seem at all interested in Dewey; however, he can't help wanting to get to know her – however astonishingly she dresses and sarcastic she seems. They eventually go out on a date and Dewey begins to fall in love with Yvette, but she has already started to convince herself that they are just too different for each other. Will it ever work out?

Quick to read and very witty, this book is definitely aimed at teenagers. It isn't the standard love story you might expect. I thought some parts were very amusing.

Sarah Barnes (13), Inverness Royal Academy

The Past
A Pistol in Greenyards by Mollie Hunter
When the people in his village are brutally evicted from their land and a member of his family is threatened by the sheriff, Connal, a young Highlander, pulls out a gun . . . an act punishable by death. Based on an actual event in the 1850s, this is about Connal's life in hiding and his attempts to save his friends from punishment.

A brilliant story – you can read, or devour, this wonderful book in one sitting.

Mark Frederick (13), The King's School

Future Worlds
A Place To Scream by Jean Ure
Set in the year 2015, this book is about Gillian, who wants so much more than your ordinary sit-down office job. With unemployment rapidly increasing, Gillian is sacked and she struggles to find a job which she will enjoy, while standing up for her rights.

This book is full of different views about life and love. It is powerfully written . . . and really makes you think about what the future could be like.

Lindsay MacPhail (13), Inverness Royal Academy

Science Fiction
Memoirs of a Dangerous Alien by Maggie Prince
The catalysts of this adventure are Dominic's new neighbours. While exploring their house he stumbles across, or, rather, is stumbled upon by a rapidly decaying corpse. No sooner has he informed the police than he is whisked off to Alpha Centauri Interchange to have his brain processed. Once in space he discovers a sinister and frightening plot to cut off Earth from the rest of the universe.

From the first page this story was full of mystery and strange happenings. It has a fast-moving, exciting storyline which keeps you in suspense.

Anne Osborne (13), Poynton County High School

Fantasy
Northern Lights by Philip Pullman
This time Lyra's curiosity has got her into more trouble than she could have ever imagined when she becomes involved with the General Oblation Board (known as the Gobblers) who are masterminding the disappearance of children from all over Britain. During her quest to save the children and with the aid of a curious device, she discovers many things about herself she never would have believed were true . . .

This book is set in a universe much like ours, yet so incredibly different. Everyone has his or her own Daemon, a kind of pet which is an extension of the person . . . it is where witches really do exist and where (from our point of view) there is a strange mix of old and new technologies. I eagerly await the next book in the trilogy.

Andrew Waghorn (15), Baines School

Horror
The Last Vampire by Christopher Pike
What do you think a vampire story should be like? Vampires hunting at night and sucking blood from anyone they meet so that they die? Well, this story is slightly different. The vampire hunts night and day. To feed, she does not have to kill. She thinks that nobody knows her secret but she, herself, is being hunted.

Scary! Christopher Pike has created a wonderful beast, different and strange.

Naomi Squires (12), Poynton County High School

Mysteries
Colour Her Dead by Celia Rees
Jude, faced with her A-level history project, decides to investigate a brutal murder which took place in the summer of 1968 in the village of Coombe Ashleigh. She begins to delve into the past, only to discover that the village community clams up about what happened on that fateful day two decades ago. The more she finds out, the more hostile the villagers become. Someone does not want the truth to come out.

This book is gripping and fast-moving with a good underlying storyline and many cleverly worked-out red herrings . . . and a twist at the end.

Tim Morgan (14), Thomas Telford School

The Supernatural
The Place Between by Hugh Scott

This is a haunting tale of people getting caught in a parallel universe, identical to our own. The antique shop-owner's daughter falls in love with a boy she has known all her life. Together they try to solve the mystery of Boskey Wood and the strange events happening there.

I thoroughly enjoyed this story for its originality in plot and setting.

Nina Bennion (15), Sir E. Scott School

Thrillers
The Kidnapping of Suzie Q by Catherine Sefton

Suzie Q is taken hostage when she gets caught up in a supermarket robbery which goes wrong. The story tells of her attempts to survive and to free herself from the remote mountain hideout where she is held hostage for weeks.

The story moves along quickly and has a nice balance of drama, tension and suspense. The robbers, too, emerge as interesting characters, as a relationship develops between Suzie and her captors.

Donald Mackay (12), Sir E. Scott School

VIEWPOINT

What sets Teenage Fiction apart from adult fiction is that they are all, without exception, written through a teenager's eyes. Note Bonnie McLellan's opening comments about the book *Do-Over*. 'I enjoyed this book immensely *because it is written from a teenager's point-of-view* . . .' This question of viewpoint is incredibly important for teenagers. It allows them to identify with the text and to *believe* in what they are reading.

Orion Books were right to publish *Sophie's World* as an adult book, but not just because it would reach a wider audience that way. Let's compare the opening of *Sophie's World* with the opening of *The Outsiders* by S. E. Hinton (written when he was just seventeen himself). They both open with the main character walking home – but see how different walking can be!

Sophie Amundsen was on her way home from school. She had walked the first part of the way with Joanna. They had been discussing robots. Joanna thought the human brain was like an advanced computer. Sophie was not certain she agreed. Surely a person was more than a piece of hardware? . . .

It was early May. In some of the gardens the fruit trees were encircled with dense clusters of daffodils. The birches were already in pale green leaf.

It was extraordinary how everything burst forth at this time of year! What made this great mass of green vegetation come welling up from the dead earth as soon as it got warm and the last traces of snow disappeared?

(*Sophie's World*)

When I stepped out into the bright sunlight from the darkness of the movie house, I had only two things on my mind: Paul Newman and a ride home. I was wishing I looked like Paul Newman – he looks tough and I don't – but I guess my own looks aren't so bad. I have light brown, almost-red hair, and greenish-grey eyes. I wish they were more grey because I hate most guys that have green eyes, but I have to be content with what I have. My hair is longer than a lot of boys wear theirs, squared off in back and long at the front and sides, but I am a greaser and most of my neighbourhood rarely bothers to get a haircut. Besides, I look better with long hair.

(*The Outsiders*)

Hinton's extract is in the first person, which gives it an immediate advantage as far as allowing the reader to get into the main character's head – but there's more to it than that. Gaarder's text is beautifully, evocatively, written – but it is obviously written by an adult pretending to think as a teenager. You can tell this from the difference in the main characters' preoccupations. Sophie is contemplating the vegetation – an adult preoccupation – whereas

Hinton's Ponyboy is contemplating himself – a very teenage pre-occupation, as anyone with teenage children will appreciate!

This question of viewpoint can lead to another criticism of teenage fiction that sometimes, particularly when writing about serious subjects, the negative side of life is glossed over in favour of the positive.

Berlie Doherty's *Dear Nobody*, the story of an unplanned teenage pregnancy, won the Carnegie Medal and is generally accepted as being a fine piece of writing. However, it has its critics, who find it disturbing that young schoolgirls should be encouraged to regard it as acceptable to become parents. The book does end on rather a positive note, given the gravity of the situation and any concerns over the future of either baby or Mum remain unarticulated. Says Helen, the young mother, after her baby is born: 'A baby isn't the end of everything. It's the beginning of something else.'

Contrast that with Margaret Drabble's *adult* book on illegitimate birth, *The Millstone*, where the baby is born halfway through the action, leaving the narrator plenty of time to conclude that, 'It was a bad investment.'

My own feelings as an editor are that Teenage Fiction is most successful when it strikes a balance. Teenagers don't want to listen to moral lectures – they want to find out what's right and wrong for themselves, and they aren't going to read/buy books which are too 'preachy' and seem to dictate a code of behaviour. On the other hand, they want a healthy dose of realism in their reading; they're starting to live in the adult world, and they don't want writers to show them a version of reality in which unpleasant truths are examined through rose-tinted spectacles. It's perfectly possible to convey a serious message in a positive way.

LENGTH

Many writers feel that, because it is written for an older market, Teenage Fiction must be much longer than a book for the under twelves. In fact, nothing could be further from the case. Judith Elliott said of *Sophie's World* that 'its length – over 400 pages – dictated a cover price of £16.99 which meant it would be well outside the normal children's market price range'.

So, as with Stand-Alone Fiction for 8–12 year-olds, it is rare for a publisher to take on Teenage Fiction over 40,000 words. Too short a book, however, is often viewed as insubstantial, not offering enough of a challenge or value for money.

My advice to a new writer working on a teenage novel would be to aim at a word count of around 30,000 words – unless writing for the Series market, in which case the Series itself will often dictate the length. Which brings me to:

TEENAGE READING SERIES

There is a distinct difference between the Stand-Alone Teenage Fiction we have been talking about so far, and Series Fiction for the same age group. Teenage Reading Series work in much the same way as the Reading Series markets we discussed in Chapter Two, in that books about similar subjects are published under an all-embracing Series title and are usually written to a fairly specific brief. The emphasis for all Reading Series is on an easy and readable writing style. Publishers are always keen to find new authors who can produce titles for this genre.

Scholastic's Point books are probably the best known Teenage Series. They have sold in their millions and, as well as the original Point Horror, there is now Point Romance, Point Crime and Point Fantasy. They are aimed at 10–13-year olds and are around 30,000 words in length.

The resurrected Livewire series (disappeared from the shelves for a while) published by Women's Press is another popular series. Originally aimed very much at the older end of the teenage market, Livewire titles used to explore controversial issues such as rape and sexual abuse. However the more recent Livewire books have been toned down a little although they are still rooted in reality, confronting problems with which teenagers can easily identify.

Making Out and *Making Waves* by Katherine Applegate are another two series aimed at the 12+ market. Published by Macmillan, titles in these series tell of a group of high school friends sharing fun, friendship – and falling in love.

Sadly, too many people dismiss this type of Series Fiction as 'escapism'. Speaking as a well-read, educated person who devours adult literary escapism books and enjoys it enormously, I take exception to this elitist attitude. I see no reason why I should have to apologise for my reading habits and, similarly, I see no reason why teenagers should be submitted to such intellectual snobbery.

I was recently telephoned by Disgusted of Tunbridge Wells. She had read an article in a Sunday newspaper which stated that it didn't matter if children read bus tickets, so long as they were reading. She objected to this attitude and wanted to quote me in her letter of reply to the newspaper, denigrating what she described as 'rubbish'. Needless to say I refused to do so. Let teenagers read bus tickets if they want to: let them read pop magazines, let them read escapist rubbish, or hopefully, the classics – but for goodness sake, don't take away their freedom of choice. It's a question of 'horses for courses' – and as you know, you can lead a horse to water but you can't make him drink. Teenagers aren't inclined to be forced into activities against their will; reading a book of any description, no matter how 'rubbishy' by adult standards, is surely better than being stimulated by nothing other than the latest computer game. All written material engenders an affection for and understanding of words and how they can be used to best effect. And the wider variety of books teenagers want to read, the more opportunities that exist for the new writer! To make this a valid part of the book rather than a separate debate, you might like to emphasise that writers shouldn't feel ashamed of writing something that isn't 'quality', or educational.

Of course, teenagers should be encouraged to broaden their reading horizons. Teenage Series writer, Dennis Hamley, writing in *Books for Keeps* (July 1995), makes an extremely valid point on this very subject:

> I don't want to sound 'teacherish', but there's a real way in which books for young people enable them to tackle more complex and demanding texts later . . . If a reader comes to *Death Penalty* (a Point Crime title) because of the football and leaves with the start of a taste for Ruth Rendell and Colin Dexter, I'll be well pleased . . . After all, 'in my father's house are many mansions' and there are just as

many routes to the ideal goal of a society of discriminating and critical readers. Critics carp at their peril. Evidence from the readers is overwhelming: the testimony of its writers, not just me, should be as significant.

Teenage Fiction: Exercises

- Pay a visit to your local children's library or bookshop and have a look at Scholastic's Point books.
- Decide which subject area is best suited to your skills – i.e. horror, fantasy, crime or romance – and come up with an idea for a book of your own.
- Start writing the first chapter (you don't have to complete it at this stage) trying to establish an upbeat, pacey, readable writing style.

CHAPTER SIX

THE SHORT STORY, MAGAZINES AND COMICS

SHORT STORIES

Not so long ago I ran a one-day seminar 'Writing Children's Books and Short Stories'. It quickly became apparent that many new writers are not aware of any difference between the two: a children's book is short; a children's short story is more of the same, but possibly shorter still.

The most obvious shortcoming of this argument is that not everything written for children is short. Novels for older children are, by adult standards, short, but at 20,000 words or more they can in no way be described as a short story. Books for younger children are short but, as I firmly told one delegate at the seminar, there is a huge difference between writing a short children's *book* and writing a short story.

'Really?' she queried. 'Why?'

At which point I was stopped in my tracks. What exactly *is* the difference between, for example, a 300-word Reader and a 3000-word short story?

Chapters for one thing. Most 3000-word books have chapters, breaking the story up into episodes, whereas a 3000-word short story is a continuous piece of text.

Nancy Smith, in her excellent book *The Fiction Writer's Handbook* describes writing the short story as being rather like 'taking a day trip somewhere, when there is no time to deviate from your destination. The novel, on the other hand, is more akin to a fortnight's holiday during which you can wander off the main route to admire the scenery, visit other places of interest, if you so desire.'

Nancy was talking about adult writing; I'm not absolutely sure that, when writing for children, there is ever much time to deviate from the main path. However, she has a point: a children's short story has to get to the point in one episode, whereas a children's short book has more scope.

Dick King-Smith's short book *Clever Duck* is about a bright young duck named Damaris who teams up with her sheepdog friend, Rory, to rid the farmyard of the pigs who have plagued their lives for so long. The story takes place over a period of time. Chapter Three opens: 'Now in summer-time some months later . . .'

This time span would not be possible in a children's short story which, as a general rule, takes place during a very short period of time. To quote Nancy Smith again: 'The short story is always concerned with a small but significant incident in the life of the main character.'

So in a short *story* by Dick King-Smith – very much the same sort of length as *Clever Duck* – 'The Rats of Meadowsweet Farm' (from the short story anthology *Muck and Magic* Stories from the countryside) the author deals with the rats' revenge on Farmer Green for massacring thirty of their population. Unlike *Clever Duck*, this story takes place over a single night.

Obviously a certain amount of background information will need to be included in any short story to explain, and set up, the plot. This is usually best done using little anecdotes interspersed with the main text.

For example take the opening of the following story:

'Closed or closed?' said Mum, standing by the little window in Katie's attic bedroom, one hand on the rusty latch.

'Closed,' mumbled Katie, sinking down under her duvet so that only her eyes peeped out over the top.

Mum laughed and let the curtains drop back. She'd asked the same question every night since they'd moved. She thought it was funny. Katie didn't. She didn't think it was funny at all.

'Perhaps Dad'll have time to fix it this weekend,' said Mum, still smiling.

Katie shook her head and sank down a little further. She didn't want Dad to fix it. Not this weekend. Not ever.

From this we learn that Katie has moved house and that, for some reason yet to be discovered, Katie is frightened of something outside her new home and doesn't want her window opened under any circumstances. All the relevant background detail has been filled in without holding up the main body of the story.

Markets

Having tried to define the short story I am now going to be very irritating and tell you that the market for children's short stories is very small.

Short story collections by one author are hard to sell unless the author is already well known. For this reason children's publishers are reluctant to take on this type of book from new writers. However, it has been known. Malorie Blackman was a new writer when she had her collection of teenage short stories, *Not So Stupid!*, accepted by Women's Press for their Livewire series. But be warned – you face an uphill struggle.

If you are intent on trying to get a collection of short stories accepted I would suggest giving them some sort of 'theme'. The stories in *Not So Stupid!* all feature girls who are, in some way, fighting back at society.

Short story collections about one *character* will probably stand a better chance of success than a random collection on a particular subject. Piccadilly Press, for example will consider a collection of stories featuring a single character – but they do stress that, for stories like this to work, it is important to give that main character a great deal of thought. *Betsey's Birthday Surprise*, again by Malorie Blackman (Piccadilly Press), is an excellent example of a successful short story collection about a single character (a little girl living in the Caribbean).

While scouring the bookshelves of your local children's bookshop or library you will notice that even short story anthologies (i.e. a collection of stories by a number of different authors) are almost always themed in some way. For example,

Snake on the Bus (Mammoth) is a collection of pet stories; and *Best of Friends* (Methuen) is a collection of stories exploring the value of friendship. Both these collections are edited by Valerie Bierman a well-known writing name in the children's publishing world. A short story anthology will still feature one name on the cover – that of the editor. Editors chosen for this task are usually high-profile as it is their name which will sell the book. Editors like Valerie usually work together with a staff editor from whichever publishing house is involved.

Author Tony Bradman is another reputable editor of short story collections. His best-known collections (for Transworld) have so far featured Space stories, Adventure stories, Sports stories, Creepy stories and Football stories. He works with a number of publishers and, encouragingly, is always keen to include new writers in his anthologies as well as more famous names.

Wendy Cooling, Chris Powling and Pat Thompson are other popular editorial names in the short story anthology genre with Pat Thompson being particularly renowned for her anthologies themed for a certain age group: *A Bus Full of Stories for Four Year Olds* (Corgi) is one example.

If you don't have an agent I would suggest getting in touch with the editors direct, via their publishers. They may then include you on their mailing lists and send you details of anthologies in preparation. I know several authors who have successfully placed work in this way.

MAGAZINE SHORT STORIES

Twenty years ago writers were spoiled for choice when it came to placing short stories in children's comics and magazines. Publishing houses such as IPC and DC Thomson were falling over each other in the mad rush to publish titles for children and teenagers. Remember *Tammy, Mandy, Bunty, Blue Jeans, Jackie, Oh Boy! My Guy, Photo-Love, Photo Secret-Love, Girl, She, Hers, Loving* . . .? The list went on and on.

Today, however, the picture is rather bleaker. There are still plenty of magazines out there, together with a handful of comics. But the opportunities they present are very different. Magazines such as *My Guy* are no longer weekly extravaganzas of romantic short-story fiction, but monthly publications featuring articles on lifestyle topics and the music world, with the occasional piece of fiction thrown in for light relief.

If you're determined to write stories for the magazine market, go into a large newsagency and have a good, long browse. Buy any titles which interest you and get a feel for the sort of profile they are trying to achieve. Most importantly read the fiction, making a careful note of word counts and subject matter. There's no earthly point in writing a 3000-word story about a marital affair if all the readers are fourteen or under and the magazine has no more than 3000 words in total!

It's helpful to contact the magazines you have chosen to target in writing or by phone and see if they issue editorial guidelines. Many magazines are more than happy to receive such requests, as they are keen to avoid having to wade through piles of unsuitable material. Guidelines generally give you a reader profile (male or female, age, whether at school, working, etc, what type of reading material he/she might favour) and then go on to specify what they are looking for in terms of a publishable story (number of characters, amount of dialogue, themes and so on).

Stories with some kind of twist are popular with many magazines. One I wrote very early on in my writing career (for *Loving* magazine) told the story of a judo fight – the twist was that the two fighting were girlfriend and boyfriend . . . 'Tricking' the reader into thinking that a couple don't know each other when they do is a well-worn concept and you will see it repeated again and again. It doesn't matter how often you repeat a theme, so long as you give it a sufficiently different angle each time, ensuring that the 'twist' continues to surprise. And no matter whether your short story has a 'twist in the tale' or not, the reader should never be able to guess the ending with complete certainty.

PHOTOSTORIES AND COMICS

Another fiction market which, like the magazine short story, has experienced a decline over the past fifteen years is the 'photostory' and 'picture-strip' market. Photostories are stories told in a series of photographs with accompanying speech 'bubbles';

picture-strips are stories told in a series of drawn images with accompanying speech 'bubbles' and/or text.

One of the reasons for the decline of photostories is that they cost a lot of money to produce. As well as the writer, models and a photographer are required, not to mention location fees, costume charges and printing costs.

However, there are still a few magazines around containing the odd photostory and many people in the publishing world believe that there will, at some stage, be a resurgence in this type of graphic story. Writing a photostory is actually quite similar to writing plays and screenplays, so if writing drama is one avenue you would like to explore, this practice in story-telling through dialogue and images will be very useful.

Photostories vary from magazine to magazine as far as length, style and subject matter are concerned. Unlike text stories, though, where length is judged in numbers of words, photostories are measured in 'frames'. There are six frames per page – sometimes one or two more, sometimes one or two less.

Picture-strips (comic-strips) are prepared in much the same way except, as the writer, you don't have to worry about cost. Because the pictures to illustrate your story are drawn by an artist there are no boundaries and you can let your imagination run riot. One word of warning though – check the nationality of the artist. When I wrote for the comic *Tammy* all the artwork was done in Spain, where graphic styling is very different. The interpretation of my picture descriptions could sometimes be unusual to say the least!

Below are the first four frames from a photostory written for a *Photo-Live* annual. This is how the original manuscript looked:

Dangerous Image

1

Beth and Anna in a living room. Anna has just come into the room and is propping up a pair of skis against the wall. She looks sneeringly over at Beth. Beth is sitting down looking up at her defensively.
TOP PANEL: The tension has been growing for days . . .
ANNA: God, Beth – sitting around as usual! You're incredible . . .

BETH: Just shut up, Anna. I don't even know why I ever agreed to come on this skiing holiday with you . . .

2

Closing in on Beth and Anna. Anna is standing close to Beth now, hands on hips. Beth is getting angrier.
BETH: I really was fool enough to think we could get on!
ANNA: How can we get on when you obviously hate my guts?

3

Beth is looking away from Anna at point on floor. Shoot looking up at Beth from below so that Anna is standing behind her. Beth looks sad and bitter. Anna is raising her eyes to the ceiling in exasperation.
BETH: Well, are you surprised after what you did to me? You – my own twin sister!
ANNA: Oh, God, we're not going to go through all that again, are we?

4

Beth has leapt to her feet and is face on to Anna, shouting at her angrily. Anna looks taken aback.
BETH: Well, why shouldn't I go through it again? You've stolen the only man I've ever loved . . .
ANNA: Oh, Beth, do you think I ever really wanted him?

Once the script is finished the story is ready to shoot.

While writing this section I've had great fun looking back through the old photostory magazines and annuals I worked on all those years ago, picking out now-famous faces. This type of modelling work is very popular as a means of subsistence of up-and-coming actors: Tracey Ullman, for example, supplemented her income during her early career by doing photostories. But like the actors and models, writers are not going to make their fortune from writing photostories – or any other type of children's short story. Compared to writing a short children's book, children's short story writing does not pay well. Payment for short stories accepted for anthologies is usually made on a flat fee basis and can rarely be described as generous. However, having a short story accepted often provides the first taste of publishing success for many writers. The short story can provide an excellent leg-up on to the first rung of the publishing ladder.

Short Story: Exercise

- Pay a visit to your local children's bookshop or library and select a short story anthology. Imagine you have been asked to write a story for the anthology concerned and see what you come up with.
- Pay a visit to your local newsagent and select a teenage magazine which contains short story fiction. Contact the editorial department and ask if they produce editorial guidelines. Write a story sticking to those guidelines (if they don't provide guidelines, follow the example of other stories in the magazine).
- In a similar way, compose a story suitable for a children's comic or photostory, following the house style of the publication you have chosen.

CHAPTER SEVEN

NON-FICTION

One of the most original and exciting submissions I have seen on a 'slush pile' arrived late one afternoon in a large cardboard suitcase. It was filled with twenty pairs of hand-made, paper shoes, which I and my colleagues spent an extremely enjoyable couple of hours examining, admiring and trying on.

The submission was entitled *The Paper Shoe Book*, by Chris Knowles and Julian Horsey. As well as the suitcase of shoes the authors had supplied two dummy books – one targeted at children, one at adults. The books supplied everything the reader needed for making their own pair of paper shoes (except for pencil, felt-tips, scissors and glue).

Sadly it wasn't right for our list. At our suggestion, however, the authors took their idea to a packager who, in turn, sold the book to Random House where it was published under their specialist books imprint, Ebury Press.

I tell this story because it highlights a number of points which should be taken into account when trying to break into the children's non-fiction market.

WHO ARE YOU WRITING FOR?

The first point to consider is what, exactly, your market consists of – i.e. who is your book for. Are there any other similar books available in bookshops and libraries? Is your book sufficiently original.

The authors of *The Paper Shoe Book* certainly considered their market carefully but, by targeting their proposal at both adults *and* children, they aimed too wide. Eventually this particular book was marketed as an adult novelty title, rather than a book for children.

Another question which you should always ask yourself when considering a book idea is 'why?' Why a book on paper shoes, for example? When Chris Knowles appeared on morning TV to promote the book he was asked exactly that question. His answer was 'Why not?', but it's more complicated than that.

During our afternoon of trying on Chris and Julian's creations it became apparent that a number of my colleagues had tried to make 'shoes' as children. And that suggests that there is a definite market for such a book.

Chris and Julian exploited the book's 'unique selling point' (often referred to as the USP) and they also, by chance or design, came up with an idea that would appeal to an international market. Last thing I heard they were off to America on a promotional tour. Non-fiction often knows no boundaries of language or culture.

Do always check out the existing market by exploring local libraries and bookshops. A quick phone call to the Young Book Trust in Wandsworth never goes amiss (see page 166). They stock every mainstream children's book published over the past two years and their library is well worth a visit.

Is It Different?

The Paper Shoe Book was certainly different. It isn't every day that a large suitcase of paper shoes lands on my desk!

However, it isn't only the appearance of the proposal that has to be original and eye-catching. The author of children's non-fiction has to find unique ways of approaching familiar subjects by giving them new angles and new perspectives.

The picture concept is vital. The difference between a good non-fiction idea and a bad one often comes down to the quality of the artwork. The author should consider carefully how the pictures and text will work together most effectively.

A novelty idea like *The Paper Shoe Book* may seem very original but this doesn't mean it is saleable. Chris and Julian were lucky but, generally speaking, new writers should steer clear of novelty books. Novelty books don't have a great sales track record overall and publishers don't like taking chances on a new author. Try to come up with a really strong and different book idea that *isn't* novelty: that has practical, factual information and an educational purpose as well as entertainment value.

Take *Everyday Machines* by John Kelly, Davie Burnie and Obin which takes a detailed look at household items such as hair dryers, vacuum cleaners, toilet tanks . . . Sounds a bit boring, doesn't it? Who'd want to buy a book about *toilet tanks*? But the book is colourful and exciting, devoting a full spread to each item, and children can have fun as they learn. Equal attention is paid to the visual image and the text.

Almost any book can look good if large amounts of money are poured into its production. But few publishers are in a position to be so profligate. A number of publishers are bringing out smaller format non-fiction titles with not a hint of colour in sight. Piccadilly Press have become well-known for their self-help books for children – self-help books with a difference, with titles like: *Four Weddings, A Funeral and When You Can't Flush the Loo*: teenage tips and tactics by Jane Goldman; *I Looked in the Mirror and Screamed*: healthier eating for teenagers by Dr Linda Ojeda; *Staying Cool, Surviving School*: secondary school strategies by Rosie Rushton.

These books combine witty titles with a lively text and are presented in a style which is easily digestible and visually stimulating. The days of having to wade through long, unbroken passages of text in order to hunt down factual information are long gone and anyone wanting to write for the children's non-fiction market should aim to make their subject matter as tempting to the reader as possible.

Like everything else, non-fiction children's books have their fads and fashions. At the time of writing it is the received wisdom that natural history and science books, together with history, have been 'done to death'. Having said that, there is always room for a genuinely new approach. Scholastic are doing particularly well with their *Horrible Science* Series – *Ugly Bugs and Blood, Bones and Body Bits* – and their *Horrible Histories* – *The Blitzed Brits* and *The Groovy Greeks* – because they are original, attractive and extremely accessible.

The Author

A common misconception amongst new writers is that the children's non-fiction market is only open to 'experts'. This is quite definitely not the case. Chris Knowles, for example, worked for London Transport prior to making his big break with *The Paper Shoe Book*.

Whilst you can allocate yourself an area of expertise and market yourself as a writer with a sound knowledge of a particular subject, never lose sight of the fact that you are not selling yourself, but your idea. The publisher's priority, after all, is to sell a creative concept to the general public, who you are is irrelevant.

Having said that, you must be able to write. It is the actual writing skills involved in children's non-fiction that many authors find difficult and lack of clarity is the biggest problem. The new author needs to have a perceptive overview of the whole book before starting; 'clarity of vision' is the key phrase. The book must be coherent and cohesive in all its elements: design, artwork and text. Artistic awareness is possibly more essential in this branch of children's writing than in any other.

When submitting ideas to a publisher, don't be precious with them. Publishers are professionals – they won't plagiarise your creativity. It is better to submit a list of a dozen or more ideas to prove that you are versatile and blessed with a fertile imagination. Remember, though, that if you are submitting several proposals you need to keep them as concise as possible.

Packagers

Packagers operate in a different way to publishers and are often more receptive to novelty books because the way they sell their product means that they can afford the high expenses involved in producing such books.

Books like *The Paper Shoe Book* go way beyond the cost parameters set by traditional publishers for their own markets. The packager, on the other hand, matches the expertise of specialist writers, artists and photographers with the professional craftsmanship of in-house editors and art editors, and then recoups the cost of the 'package' by pre-selling rights in the titles to publishers throughout the world: what is known as a 'co-edition'.

Co-editions are often complicated to produce and manage, because of the time and co-ordination involved, so specialist knowledge of how they work is vital.

There are a number of packagers dealing in children's books and a comprehensive up-to-date list can be found in *The Writers' & Artists' Yearbook* and *The Writers' Handbook*.

Growth Areas

Those writers who are keen to break into children's non-fiction should be encouraged by the fact that this sector of the market has seen huge growth over the past five years.

The National Curriculum has set guidelines for what is to be taught and when, and publishers are now able to produce non-fiction books to fit in with those requirements. Many publishers' lists, previously dominated by fiction, now have separate non-fiction departments with strong and expanding non-fiction programmes.

Dorling Kindersley broke the mould of traditional non-fiction and many other publishers are following their lead whilst, at the same time, pursuing new directions of their own.

MAGAZINES

There are a number of children's and teenage magazines on the market which depend upon freelance contributions.

One recent publishing sensation has been the launch of *Girl Talk*. This magazine made a departure from the usual comic-style approach of publications for this age group, and offered something more in line with teenage magazines but for a much younger age group (seven/eight to tennish).

It is published by the BBC and, as one would expect with the backing of a broadcasting organisation, is highly illustrated, brightly coloured, glossy and busy. It features pullout pictures of cute and cuddly animals mixed with book reviews, snippets of interesting information and fiction (text and photo-stories).

For example in one issue (at the time of writing) there is a spread featuring a reader's 'Dream Come True', an article on Anteaters, a feature entitled '20 ways to say hello', instructions on how to make a balloon fish, a recipe for bread bears, plus fiction, puzzles and competitions.

A similar magazine for boys is *Boys 1st*. Editor-in-Chief is mother-of-three, Christine Cubitt, who launched the magazine after vainly scouring the magazine racks for reading matter that would bridge the gap, for boys, between *The Beano* and football magazines. When she couldn't find anything she decided to publish something herself.

The resulting *Boys 1st* was launched in March 1997 with a 10,000 print run, to be distributed in the North of England only. However, it caught on and is now being distributed nationwide and has a current print run of 30,000.

The magazine is a wholesome mix of fact and fun for eight to thirteen year olds. There's science, dinosaurs and cars, comic strip and star interviews.

Setting the editorial agenda came naturally to Christine.

She says, 'Editorial has to be informative and involving – boys don't read very well and have to be pushed at that age, so it has to be visual, original and contemporary. Also we want to educate them, but we have to disguise it as fun. What I'm trying to do is show boys that by being determined and focused on what they want to do, they can achieve it.'

As well as fun-based material for children there are also a few more educational titles on the market – most sold by subscription only.

Aquila is an attractive and colourful magazine described as being 'the magazine for children who enjoy challenges'. This magazine mainly features educational puzzles and quizzes, mixed with informative features, author interviews, letters, book reviews, jokes and competitions.

Bayard Press, in conjunction with HarperCollins, publish three small format magazines aimed at three different age groups. *Collins Story Box* is for three to six year olds and is designed to be read aloud to children. It features an illustrated story, topical features, the adventures of two characters called Charlotte and Henry plus games and activities.

Collins Adventure Box is for six to nine year olds and is an exciting combination of facts and fiction for children beginning to read on their own. *Collins Discovery Box* is for eight to twelve year olds and is a treasure-trove of discoveries all about animals, science, history and people from all around the world.

Along similar lines to *Discovery Box, Wildside* is a brand-new magazine for children. This is distributed direct into schools and, as the title suggests, is a magazine concerned with wildlife and environmental issues. It is targeted at eight- to- twelve-year-old boys and girls.

Publisher, Annah Ouamira, wants the magazine to offer interesting facts in a fun way. She is keen to find writers who can speak directly to children in a way that they will understand. She feels it is important that children can relate to the fact presented to them in the magazine.

She explains, 'If, for example, we are talking about the Emperor Penguin, something like a size comparison will be important so that a child can really visualise just how large these birds are.'

As mentioned in the previous chapter, there are also plenty of magazines around for older children and teenagers. At the time of going to press there was *Girl Talk, Just Seventeen, Shout, Mizz, Sugar, Bliss, Mademoiselle* . . . the list goes on. All are targeted almost exclusively at girls and are a mixture of lifestyle advice and pop gossip, with the odd bit of fiction thrown in for good measure.

However, anyone wanting to write non-fiction articles for these magazines should speak to the editorial team concerned first. Often this type of magazine will originate ideas in-house and only commission pieces from writers already known to them; or it will have a team of staff writers who provide all the non-fiction copy.

It is essential to study the magazines in depth, to enable you to be in touch with the wishes and desires of today's young girl. Many 1990s magazines feature non-fiction pieces with titles like 'Drugs Forced Me to Abort My Baby' (*Just Seventeen*) and 'What's Your Seduction Style? (*Bliss*). So that piece on 'Crocheting for Beginners' which has been gathering dust at the bottom of your desk drawer, just won't find a home in the marketplace.

You may not approve, or even want to write, this sort of material – but, judging by the sales figures of these magazines, this is what your average young girl wants, so this is what publishing companies will ensure that they get. As writers it's important we understand the market as it is and not as it should be. Publishers are *not* charities and they will continue to publish what sells whether we, as writers, like it or not.

Non-Fiction: Exercises

- Select an object which you use during your everyday routines – preferably something which children use as well. This can be something as simple as a comb, or something more complex like a computer.
- Think of ways in which you could write about your chosen object, looking at it from as many different perspectives as possible.
- Now see if you can develop your idea into a full-length book idea. For example, if you chose a comb, perhaps you could consider making it part of a book on hair and hairstyles.
- If you feel you have come up with a winning concept do some research in your local children's library or bookshop to see if anything similar is already available.

CHAPTER EIGHT

POETRY

My poem's enclosed
for you to see.
If they're worth printing
talk to me.
Give me a ring
to fix a date.
We'll set a time
Please don't be late.
If you aren't impressed, however
return to sender.
I'll put them out
again to tender!

This witty ditty landed on my desk, along with several poems. It certainly made me laugh and the accompanying poems were of good quality. But as an editor I needed to know more – a *lot* more – before I could even start to consider these poems seriously.

AGE RANGE

The poetry editor, once he/she has decided that a collection of poems has potential, will first of all consider the age range for which the author is writing. Those of you who think poetry should be ageless are right: good poetry can be enjoyed right across the board. Elderly people still enjoy nursery rhymes; very young children will often display a surprisingly sophisticated taste in poetry. However, it is important that the poet has some sort of target audience in mind.

Generally speaking children's poetry can be divided into three distinct categories: poetry for the 6–10 age range, poetry for the 10–12 age range, and teenage/young adult poetry. Poetry for the under-sixes tends to be published in the form of 'picture books' rather than straightforward poetry. (It is also worth mentioning, at this point, that teenage poetry is a small market – and extremely hard to enter.)

EXPERIENCE

Having assessed the age range for which the poet is writing, the next big stumbling block is experience. By this I don't, necessarily, mean publishing experience – but it obviously helps if your poetry has had some kind of a public airing, in magazines, newspapers or through small presses.

Many of today's top children's poets wrote for adults before they moved into the children's arena. Certainly it is fair to say that you are probably doomed to failure. In order to be taken seriously it is important to show publishers that you are a 'Poet' with a capital 'P' and that you are committed to your chosen artform. Otherwise not only will you find that there are limited openings but, also, that you do not have the correct credentials deemed necessary to make it in the world of poetry. For example, John Aigard and Jackie Kay were both published by Blood Axe (a long-established and well-respected adult poetry small press) prior to being published by Penguin Children's Books.

The Poetry Society (22 Betterton Street, London WC2H 9BU) is an excellent resource for the new poet. They too stress the importance of gaining experience before approaching publishers, saying – and I quote – 'no publisher is going to go near an unknown name'.

They suggest building up a portfolio, including magazines or other publications in which your poetry has appeared and lists of reading and festivals with which you have been involved.

They provide advice on how to gain access to all those opportunities.

Membership costs £24 per year at the time of writing and for that you will receive the *Poetry Review* and *Poetry News* quarterly. The *Review* is Britain's premier poetry magazine, at the cutting edge of the poetry scene, providing a forum for new poems from both 'rookie' and established poets. Poems are included at the discretion of the editor, regardless of whether or not the author is a member of the Society.

Poetry News gives details of poetry competitions and awards. Prizes for such competitions can range from thousands of pounds to a book token. Many of them produce a winners' anthology, which will inevitably end up on the desk of poetry editors.

It is particularly interesting to note that the Poetry Society's information sheet on children's poetry publishers only lists thirteen major names. If you consider that there are over one hundred children's book publishers it gives some idea as to the difficulty of breaking in to this particular genre.

Performance

These days the children's poet must not only enjoy performing their own poetry, but they must be good at it. They must also be prepared to commit large amounts of their time to touring schools, bookshops, libraries and festivals in order to read and promote their work. Live performance is considered to be a vital part of any poet's CV. Certainly at Penguin Children's Books, which has one of the strongest children's poetry lists in the UK including such poetic luminaries as Roger McGough, Michael Rosen, Kit Wright, Brian Patten, Benjamin Zephaniah, John Aigard, James Berry and Jackie Kay (to name but a few), the importance of performance is more or less written into the contract.

Lindsay MacRae's first collection of children's poetry, *You Canny Shove Yer Granny Off A Bus!* has just been published by Viking. She says that she started out as a performance poet of adult poetry and describes herself, back then, as 'the angry young woman' performing politically-slanted poetry in alternative cabaret clubs and pubs.

But being, first and foremost, a performer, helps MacRae to write her poetry. Reading poetry out loud helps a writer get a sense of rhythm, of which words resonate with power and emotion, of which poems are likely to earn a positive response from an audience/readership. Children respond particularly well to poems with strong rhythms, humour, and plenty of dialogue featuring characters speaking in different 'voices'. Lindsay MacRae's poems often start out as imagined conversations and develop from there:

> 'I *insist* on paying,' said Doris
> 'It's *my* treat!' shrieks Mum,
> shoving the sweaty £20 note back at her.
> '*Please* let me pay,' begs Doris,
> scrunching up the note and shoving it
> in Mum's pocket.
>
> From *High Noon at Barking Odeon*

One can easily imagine how hilarious this 'strange adult conflict' would become when performed.

MacRae does stress, however, that a contrast of styles is important and that one wildly hilarious poem after another would become wearing, even in performance. Her collection ranges from the scatological *Dog Poo Haiku* to the much more sombre and serious *Children Also Get Depressed*.

Lindsay MacRae is convinced that the fact she is young and a woman has contributed to her success in the children's poetry field. Many of today's children's writers are older men and, whilst their poetry continues to be brilliantly inspiring, there is a distinct lack of female poets and poets from multi-cultural backgrounds.

Lindsay's advice to the aspiring children's poet is to get out there and to build up a following. Build on your eccentricities and idiosyncrasies – be different. Your own personal fan club is vital to the publisher, as it proves there is a market for your work. Offer your talents to local schools and libraries. You'll soon find out if you've got what it takes to perform – and if your poems work in front of a young, live audience with very frank theories on what is boring and what isn't.

SUBMISSION

So you've won a couple of competitions, your poems have been published in a few specialist magazines, and hordes of children are besieging you, *begging* to know where they can buy your first collection. *Now* is the time to approach a publisher.

No poetry editor wants to be deluged with the entire contents of your life's work. Personally, I like to see no more than twelve poems, 'grouped' or 'themed' in some way, which can help to give your collection focus. For example, all the poems in one of Brian Patten's collections, *Utter Nutters*, are based around one particular street. It's not essential, however, to find a theme if your poems only seem to work as separate entities.

Readers of unsolicited poetry will be looking for a distinctive 'voice' which makes the poet unique. Remember that your voice has to appeal to the child of today. This question of 'voice' or 'style' is always a thorny one; even published poets agree that it is hard not to be influenced by the styles of others.

Again, examine what makes you stand out from the crowd and use those individual qualities to make you stand out. Jackie Kay, for example uses idiomatic language and the Scottish dialect to great effect:

> But see when Sleekit is discovered for her cunning wit . . .
> What does she do first? Blame it on Greta, Jimmy, Jo,
> Gillian, or worse,
> her tiny toty wee sister (shame)
> who screams in a big voice for a wee wean:
> WISNAE ME WISNAE ME WIS HER AGAIN
> WISNAE ME WISNAE ME WIS HER AGAIN
>
> From *Sleekit*

It is important that children's poets make the distinction between 'verse' and 'poetry'; children's poetry publishers are in the business of publishing saleable collections of poetry, not greeting cards! Nor are most poetry editors looking for picture-book material. One-off poems, accompanied by hand-scrawled notes asking the publisher to include it in their next poetry anthology, are out as well, I'm afraid. One-off poems by unknowns are rarely included in anthologies, unless it is a particularly specialist collection such as *A Stack of Story Poems* collected by Tony Bradman which included one poem from a completely new writer, *The Boy and the Boggart* by Ghillian Potts.

At the end of the day, what really matters is the reaction to poetry of the children themselves. Because children's poetry today is so relevant and accessible it will often provide reluctant readers with their first insight that books can be fun.

Consider the words of children's poetry anthologiser, Anne Harvey, writing in *Poetry: A Penguin Booklist*: 'Look for the best from the past and present. Offer children what will stretch imagination and add to experience, widen horizons, deepen their feelings, enliven their senses.'

Or, to put it another way:

> I would speak great poems
> With me great big voice
> Great big hugs and kisses
> Would make me feel nice
> This great world would work together
> as a team
> I would live for ever
> In me great big dream
> From *Once Upon a Time* by Benjamin Zephaniah

Poetry: Exercises

- Pay a visit to your local children's library or bookshop and have a browse through all the most recently published poetry books – collections by single poets and themed anthologies.
- Choose an anthology that you like and imagine that you have been approached to contribute one more poem to the collection. Write a poem which seems to you to fit with the mood of the collection.
- Think about your style of writing, or 'voice', and choose a subject around which you could centre your own collection of poems.

CHAPTER NINE

MULTIMEDIA AND THE INTERNET

'Don't believe in them,' one gentleman said to me recently, as I waved around the entire contents of a children's encyclopedia encapsulated on a small, shiny, round, silver disc, otherwise known as the CD-Rom. 'Be the death of the book, they will.'

I was talking to a North London writer's group and had dared to suggest that electronic publishing was one (and *only* one) way forward for the children's publisher, writer and reader. I had deliberately kept this particular section of my talk for the inevitable stage when a few members start nodding off, thinking that it might generate renewed enthusiasm. I couldn't have been more wrong! There was nothing but head-shaking and finger-wagging, accompanied by dire premonitions of doom and gloom. For this group, at any rate, the CD-Rom was seen as nothing but a threat.

CD-ROM – THE DEATH OF THE BOOK?

'Not true!' said Guy Gadney, an expert on multimedia projects within children's publishing.

Guy points out that, when photography was first developed, critics said it would be the death of art. That didn't happen. The fact is, photography is not an art form in *competition* with any-thing else: it is a valid art form in its own right and can exist happily *alongside* other forms of art. Similarly the electronic book – or CD-Rom – can operate *alongside* the printed word.

Ah, I can hear you all saying, but multimedia is different from photography. Children will just plump for the easiest option and drop everything else.

The evidence proves otherwise. Children's publishers moved into the audio market – another challenger to the printed word – some time ago, with tapes of books proving to be excellent sellers. Videos, too, have been launched as spin-offs of books or book-based material – *Thomas the Tank Engine* and *Spot the Dog* are amongst the biggest successes. Despite this, children's book sales continue to rise – by 16% in 1995, according to the Publishers' Association.

It could even be argued that audio tapes and videos actually *promote* book sales, with one complementing the other. This is also true of multimedia. Ginn and Heinemann are both bringing out CD-Rom titles aimed at being an *extension* to integral course books for early maths and early reading, rather than standing on their own in place of printed material.

What is Multimedia?

According to Dorling Kindersley (the market leaders in this field) multimedia is an amalgam of what were once separate media disciplines – words, sound, animation and video – with computer software as the 'glue' that holds them all together.

The computer software is known as the CD-Rom which stands for Compact Disc Read Only Memory. This looks just like an audio CD but 'plays' on a computer rather than a music system. It can hold more than 450 times the data stored on a conventional floppy disk and can store the equivalent of 300,000 pages of printed material.

What Does It Do?

Have you ever looked at the pages of a particularly exciting children's book and wondered what it would be like to enter that world – to literally 'walk into' the book? I know I have; I know, also, that it is something about which most children fantasise.

With the CD-Rom this dream becomes reality. CD-Rom

titles are books with which the user can interact. For example, *Peter Rabbit's Interactive World* features Beatrix Potter's exquisitely drawn watercolour illustrations come to life.

'Children must feel that they are stepping into the world of the *Tales* so that they can explore and experience it,' says Sally Floyer, Publisher at Frederick Warne. 'Our task was to work out how the settings of the different *Tales* might fit together so that the viewer moves from one panorama to the next. Where is the rabbit's fir tree in relation to Mr Jeremy Fisher's pond? Where do you find yourself if you come out of Mr McGregor's garden and turn left?'

Why Now?

So why is everyone suddenly so interested in the CD-Rom? Why am I even including a chapter on multimedia in what is, essentially, a book about *writing* for children?

Well, multimedia is going to affect us all, whether we are involved in publishing or not. In the computer industry, there is a principle 'Moore's Law' named after the co-founder of Intel. Moore predicted that the power and density of chips would continue to double, and their price halve, every eighteen months. What this means is that by the end of the century we will all have on our desks, on top of our television sets, or in our telephones, a computer as powerful as the largest mainframe in the world today.

It's hard to know just how children's publishing will be affected by all this change, but there is no doubt that it *will* be radically transformed. 'There will be incredible opportunities' says Alan Buckingham, Managing Director of Dorling Kindersley Multimedia. 'Not just to mix media (words, pictures, sound, animation, video) in ways that were traditionally outside the scope of book publishing, but to reach new audiences and to put them in touch with authors in new ways.'

PC Kids Magazine Editor, Paul Mallinson, is more cautious about the so-called multimedia revolution. He feels it is too early to tell where multimedia is going and points out that already a number of publishers have dipped their toes in the water only to get badly burnt. There is no doubt, though, that multimedia publishing is now finding itself at the centre of a web of overlapping relationships when it comes to the education arena. One entanglement centres around the various contentious efforts to reform the nation's education system, and the increasing tendency of parents to adopt solutions that are outside of that system – as witnessed particularly by their increasing tendency to purchase home PCs (increasing more in Europe than the US). As a result major new market opportunities for the multimedia publisher and author are being created.

Any writer planning to move into multimedia should, as always, do thorough market research. But where to go to view the hundreds of different products on the market?

Bookshops are still reluctant to sell multimedia products, partly due to the problems of display space, but also because selling such products requires 'book' sellers to acquire new market knowledge, and technical know-how should problems occur.

One chain of shops prepared to make the effort is Five to Twelve, which sells books, toys and educational multimedia titles all on one premises. Their staff have up-to-the-minute knowledge of the products they sell and, what's more, there are several multimedia computers available for customers to 'try out' the various titles on offer.

Pricing of CD-Rom titles remains a problem. It all has to do with 'perceived value'. To the uninitiated all CD-Rom titles look the same, whatever the quality and the depth of their content. So how do customers compare one with another, and judge that one title might be worth £59 while £19 is a fair price for another? By contrast it is very easy to flip through a book and get a sense of what it contains and whether you are getting value for money.

FICTION MULTIMEDIA

Surprising though it may seem – and exciting though it is – there is nothing particularly new about the concept of an interactive story.

Take the opening of this story being told by a parent to his/her child:

'Once upon a time there was a princess who lived in a castle, in the middle of a beautiful garden, in the middle of an enchanted forest ...'

'Does the princess live alone?'

'No. She lives with her mother and two brothers.'

'Where are they?'

'The mother is in her bedroom, and the brothers are playing darts in the Great Hall.'

'What does the mother's bedroom look like? What does the Great Hall look like? Why is the princess not playing darts too? Where is the father? What makes the garden beautiful? How is the forest enchanted?'. . .

And so on. The story has, quite spontaneously become interactive; the child is asking questions which dictate the direction in which the story will move.

This classic art of storytelling goes back hundreds of years. The linear approach to a story has been abandoned almost before it starts and this is very much what happens with fiction on CD-Rom. The first-ever story told could be classed as the original prototype for the CD-Rom, with multimedia publishing taking us back to storytelling in its very oldest form.

You could say that *Alice in Wonderland* is interactive. Alice is being presented with choices through the book (for example, 'eat me/drink me') and her decisions affect how the story progresses. Novelty-type books, such as *Spot*, depend on physical interaction and, more recently, the 'choose your own adventure' books encouraged the reader to skip backwards and forwards through the text.

It is hardly surprising, then, that many publishers of traditional children's fiction are jumping on the multimedia bandwagon. Random House have been established in this field for some time now and are well known for their Living Books series aimed at the 3–8 year-old. Each Living Book comes with the original storybook from which it was adapted. Even the traditionalist Oxford University Press have brought out CD-Rom versions of *The Fish Who Could Wish* followed closely by *Winnie the Witch* and *Dragons*.

But it isn't only the more modern children's books which have been transferred to CD-Rom. Electronic Arts produce *Jungle Book* and Ablac produce *Magic Tales*. The latter is a collection of three traditional folk tales – *Baba Yaga and the Magic Geese, Imo and the King* and *The Little Samurai* – from Russia, Africa and Japan. The most classic CD-Rom of them all, though, comes from Oxford University Press who brought out *A Christmas Story* – and you don't get much more classic than that!

NON-FICTION MULTIMEDIA

Edutainment is a horrible word but it does clearly illustrate how narrow the divide is between children's fiction and children's non-fiction multimedia publishing. Even so-called 'pure' fiction titles seek to *educate* as well as *entertain* and, in many ways, this summarises the strength of any CD-Rom title. As Marshall McLuhan said, 'Anyone who tries to make a distinction between education and entertainment doesn't know the first thing about either.'

Computers, with their interactivity and multimedia capability, can now provide a completely new kind of learning experience for children. Children are taking to this new technology without fear, and with total enthusiasm. Give a child a new, unseen CD-Rom and they will have learnt their way around it within minutes (and without the use of Help screens which, as multimedia publishers themselves admit, are entirely designed for adult use).

Certainly if there is any threat to the written word it will come from children's *non-fiction* multimedia as opposed to children's *fiction* multimedia. Children love educational computer software much more than educational books, because of its comparative richness and drama. As Alan Buckingham of Dorling Kindersley Multimedia, writes in *Publishing News*:

'The new generation of information titles can include sound, animation, video, 3D environments and even virtual worlds – all the media elements that simply can't be delivered on the printed page, and all things that make the children's experience more exciting, more compelling and, some would say, closer to that of the real world.'

Alan Buckingham has every right to say this; Dorling Kindersley produce an impressive array of non-fiction multimedia titles. Imagine owning an 'atlas' on CD-Rom which allows you to virtually 'walk in' on any country in the world; or being able to hear the joy of the German crowds as they tear down the Berlin Wall; or being able to 'time-travel' through twelve different time periods. And who could call science boring when it is possible, with CD-Rom, to see the internal workings of mechanical objects, or even the human body, animated by computer? So much more interesting than studying two-dimensional line diagrams on the page.

And, of course, non-fiction multimedia is interactive. Children immediately become active, not passive, learners. The best multimedia titles will set them assignments to perform, hidden objects to find, maps to decipher, and problems or quizzes to solve.

For example *The Adventures of Hyperman* (IBM) is an action-adventure, interactive cartoon enabling children to explore science. Hyperman must stop two 'baddies', Entrobe and his wicked sidekick Kid Chaos, from destroying the world by altering the Earth's chemical, physical and biological properties. Only Hyperman and his teen genius partner Emma C Squared can stop them by using several tools, including an electron microscope that magnifies objects and a chalkboard where diagrams are displayed to visualise experiments before they are activated.

Similarly Dorling Kindersley's Eyewitness Virtual Reality titles create a museum scenario in which items can be collected 'floor by floor' (connected by 'lift'), bringing to life an exciting, virtual environment for simple browsing or in-depth research. Clicking on any of the major exhibits accesses pop-up screens filled with exciting audio and video clips. A visit to the 'museum souvenir store' allows the child to create their own sounds and images for the desktop. There are also guided tours, sound booths, and games and activities to test your knowledge.

Dorling Kindersley and IBM are by no means the only companies producing state-of-the-art educational software. Heinemann have produced a children's encyclopedia, and Random House have a whole catalogue of educational multimedia titles with the overall title *Knowledge Adventure* – and an apt sub-title: *The Thrill of Learning Starts Here*.

WRITING MULTIMEDIA

The most famous multimedia writing success story must be *PAWS: A Personal Automated Wagging System* (A Domestic Funk Production, Virgin Records). This engaging title is described as a 'dog simulator for ages 2 to 103'. The story goes that the three authors were sitting around in a pub, sharing a pint – when inspiration struck.

As it happens these weren't just three ordinary authors in a pub: Alan Snow is a published illustrator, Nick Batt is part of a sound production team, and David Furlow is a computer programmer. But potential 'authors' of CD-Rom material don't have to possess this type of high-level expertise to come up with winning ideas.

There are, in fact, only a limited number of fiction titles suitable for the multimedia treatment. Any book being considered as a CD-Rom title must have both potential for interactivity and potential for the utilisation of a mix of different media. However, as the supply of previously published titles eventually dries up, multimedia opportunities for the children's writer and illustrator will increase.

Well-known children's illustrator Korky Paul is enthusiastic about the challenge: 'Multimedia offers children's book writers and illustrators an exciting new medium in which to express themselves. It has all the delights of an animated movie, but with that extra dimension of being interactive – and that is what makes the creative juices flow.'

Before presenting a multimedia idea to a publisher, writers should question themselves carefully. Does the idea really require the cost and technical skills of a multimedia treatment? Would it be better as a book – or a film – or a TV programme?

As I started writing this chapter my first unsolicited script specifically targeted for CD-Rom landed on my desk. The author described it to me as a 'CD-Rom talkie click and point adventure game' – I think I know what he's getting at.

But am I the right person to assess this submission? Probably not. Any publisher moving into the world of multimedia will have a separate department (even if it's only one person) dealing with this whole area. I do not mean that editors will be eliminated altogether from electronic publishing – it's just that it requires huge investment and there's no room for amateurs. To pick up, and capitalise on, an idea for a CD-Rom takes vision and commitment. *PAWS* was published as a book by Harper-Collins but they, and others, failed to see its potential for multimedia treatment. In the end a single person's vision generated an outstandingly innovative piece of work.

THE INTERNET

The formal definition of the Internet is an international computer network; the core of this network consists of computers permanently linked through high-speed connections. To join the Internet all you have to do is connect your computer to any one of these computers. Once you're 'online' (connected by way of a 'modem' through an ordinary telephone line) and can 'talk' to any other computer on the Internet, whether they're in your home town or the other side of the world.

I'm not going to go into the Internet in any great detail in this book, as it has no great significance for the new children's writer except as a method of research. However, it is worth mentioning that a few of the larger children's publishers are setting up 'homes' on the Web. Puffin Books have created the first UK Children's Book Website, aimed directly at children of 8–12 years but also containing resource material for teachers, writers and anyone else interested in children's books.

This 'site' takes the form of a colourful house, with each room corresponding to a particular aspect of Puffin publishing. For the children's writer, the Bathroom contains the start of a story (from a well-known author) which can be continued by the user on a regular basis – a sort-of international game of Consequences! And in the Library, there is a section on 'Becoming an Author' (written by me!), targeted at the adult rather than the child.

But before you go rushing off for a spot of 'surfing' (jargon for exploring the Internet) there's quite a lot of this book left to be getting on with. See you in Part Two!

II

GET WRITING!

CHAPTER TEN

SUBJECT MATTER

Once an author has studied the market they hope to write for, they must decide what they want to write *about*.

If you have studied the first part of this book carefully, and completed some of the exercises at the end of each chapter, you will, by now, have a good idea of the different types of children's book currently being sold. You may even already have decided what type of book that you want to write, or identified a gap in the market which you want to fill.

Alternatively, you may be feeling punch-drunk on the sheer enormity of the market; perhaps you are thinking that every subject under the sun has already been covered and that not even Roald Dahl himself could come up with anything new or different.

If you fall into this last category, relax. Fact is, in all probability every subject under the sun *has* already been covered. This doesn't mean, however, that there is nothing left for you to write about. Margret Geraghty, in her excellent *Novelist's Guide*, compares fiction to the fashion business: *'Just as Westwood [fashion designer] might take a plain dress and cover it with chicken wire, so can writers take a basic plot and develop it afresh.'*

WHAT CAN I WRITE ABOUT?

The first thing to do is to come up with an idea you feel really enthusiastic about and *then* worry about whether it has been done before and, if so, how it was tackled. Some writers argue that there are only a limited number of plots that human ingenuity can feasibly contrive: originality consists of 'customising' them and coming up with a new angle to satisfy the needs of the current market.

There is no doubt that, in children's publishing as in adult publishing, there are 'trends' for certain types of books. Books about forest animals may be popular one year, only to be replaced by school stories the next. There is really no easy way to get to grips with what is popular and what isn't. In Chapter 4 we looked at all the different 'types' of novel – all I can do here is point out the possible pitfalls of each, so that you are aware of the lie of the land before you start.

Historical Fiction

Because of the amount of research involved, historical fiction is probably the most arduous market of all for the children's writer. There is little point spending months working on an idea if ultimately it has mimimal chance of acceptance. Having said that, this area is slowly coming back into favour with publishers.

Time-Slip Stories

This is, perhaps, an 'accessible' way of dealing with historical issues. For example, *James Bodger and the Priory Ghost* by Gene Kemp is a riotous tale in which the twentieth century meets the Middle Ages. Whilst it contains a fair amount of historical detail, it is also a fun, contemporary read. Time-slip stories seem less popular than they used to be, however.

Fantasy

A popular area with a strong following. But *Lord of the Rings* fans beware! There are a number of highly successful writers of 'straight' fantasy around – Terry Pratchett and Susan Cooper to name but two – but it is difficult to excel in this area simply because a new fantasy novel has to compete against extremely stiff competition.

Fantasy also seems to attract extreme reactions: readers either love it or loathe it, so the market is very polarised. However, it is possible to focus on the 'non-fantasy' elements of your story to give those who 'loathe' fantasy something to hook into, while fulfilling the more specific requirements of established fantasy fans.

Science Fiction

This is another 'love it or loathe it' area, I'm afraid. On the other hand, as with fantasy, it is best to write a science fiction story which even non-believers can enjoy. The secret is to keep the storyline as non-technical as possible – too much detail about the inner workings of spaceships can be off-putting for the sceptics.

Fairy Tales

The mistake some new authors make with Fairy Tales is to update old fairy tales by giving them a modern-day slant. This has been done so often it is now hard to give any traditional story an original angle. If I could have a pound for every time I've read about a princess who likes climbing tress, or a prince who rides a motorbike rather than a horse, I'd be a rich woman!

Adventure Stories

These are plot-driven, action-based books but, too often, new writers try to imitate Enid Blyton. I'm afraid it's a question of 'been there, done that, time to move on'. Make no mistake, Blyton wrote wonderful, pacey, stream-lined stories, but today's publishers demand more than this type of one-dimensional plot. It is much better if an adventure story has some real relevance to modern life. For example Malorie Blackman's *Hacker*, as the title suggests, features computers and a girl's fight to free her father from prison – a sort of updated *Railway Children*. Catherine MacPhail's *Run Zan Run* features a girl's fight against serious bullying helped by a homeless runaway. In both these books it is the adventure which drives the plot but that doesn't stop either author from examining other issues as well.

Horror and Ghost Books

Plausibility is the biggest problem with horror and ghost books. It is all too easy to slip into melodrama which will, at best, seem funny or, at worst, ridiculous. As with adventure books the best horror and ghost stories set out to do more than just horrify or frighten – they will often explore other issues, and, in particular, the success of their plots will depend upon strong characterisation. This isn't to take anything away from the type of mass-market horror and ghost books that publishers such as Scholastic produce. Series such as *Point Horror* and *Hippo Ghost* do set out to just horrify and frighten (in the best possible taste of course!) and they are none the worse books for that. However, they are hard to get right and unless you really enjoy reading this type of book yourself I wouldn't even attempt to try.

Funny Books

Being deliberately 'funny' in writing is probably the hardest thing of all to achieve. What makes someone laugh is very personal and subjective, writers either tend to go right over the top, or are so subtle the humour gets missed. If you would like to write a funny book I suggest you look carefully at books which make you laugh and try to work out just *why* it is so humorous. Sometimes this will mean dissecting a particular sentence bit by bit; very often, it is not *what* is written but *how* it is written.

People Books

These are, essentially, character-led books. As with all children's books there must also be a good story but it is the characters that lead the story rather than the other way round. In other words the story is secondary to the main point, whatever that may be. Ruth Symes's *Master of Secrets* is an excellent example of a 'people book'. True, it is part mystery, part funny, part adventure, part romance but, as well as all these things, or perhaps *in spite* of all these things, it is a story about two boys, about their lives, their problems, their relationships and the way in which they interact with each other. The problem with writing a people book is that so often the characters can take over and 'plot' goes out the window. The result is a wonderful character study but no framework in which those characters can be contained. I think the best people books start out with a situation and develop from there, but I'm not convinced you can set out to write a people book – I think they just happen.

Taboo Areas

I would like to say that there are no taboo areas when writing children's fiction but that isn't true. What I can say is that the areas I consider to be taboo are probably not the ones you would expect.

I don't believe that there is any subject which is too 'adult' for children. Rape, incest, abuse, teenage pregnancies, drug addiction, homelessness, are all subjects which can, and should, be covered in children's fiction (though, of course, the age of the target readership has to be taken into account). Berlie Doherty's *Dear Nobody* deals with the issue of teenage pregnancy; Michelle Magorian's *Goodnight Mister Tom* deals with child abuse; Robert Swindells' *Stone Cold* deals with homelessness. And these are all award-winning books – with good reason. They deal with the issues concerned with intelligence, insight and sensitivity.

So, technically, there is no subject matter which can't be covered in children's fiction. However, there are areas which I have allocated as my own personal 'taboos'.

Talk to any children's reader or editor and you will quickly discover that there are certain book ideas which crop up time and time again on the slush pile. I have seen hundreds of variations on the *Mr Men* books, *The Shoe People* (particularly tools and fruit coming to life), *Thomas the Tank Engine* (Desmond the Dustcart/ Tommy the Tipper Truck, etc), *Fireman Sam* (the milkman is a popular alternative to the fireman) and *Animals of Farthing Wood*. Roald Dahl, Enid Blyton and Beatrix Potter imitators also crop up with alarming frequency. Recurring themes are: missing socks; supermarket trolleys coming to life; much-loved pets (particularly cats); foiled burglaries; tooth fairies; bathtime; bereavement; children being whisked up into the clouds during the night. An editor friend of mine's own personal favourite is *The Holocaust from a Hare's Point of View*. Mine is *Young Dung, the Story of a Dung Beetle*.

I could go on – but I won't. Suffice to say that these are 'taboo' areas as far as publishing is concerned.

Political Correctness

Two particular books come to my mind whenever the subject of political correctness rears its ugly head. One is *Abigail at the Beach* by Felix Pirani and the other is a book which shall remain name-less about two characters called Morris Minus and Polly Plus.

Abigail at the Beach caused the most incredible furore when it was first published in 1988. It was even discussed in the House of Commons!

A picture book, it tells the story of Abigail, who visits the beach with her father. While Dad reads his book (assisted by three cans of beer) Abigail builds 'the biggest sandcastle in the world'. When her sandcastle is threatened by three boys, two girls and a dog, Abigail threatens to get her Dad to hang two of the boys upside down by their heels, to break the other boy's arms and to frazzle his bike and to shoot holes in the dog.

The book is cleverly and realistically written with a certain tongue-in-cheek, subversive humour. The objections, however, were vociferous and concerned both the beer drinking and the violence.

This, to my mind, is political correctness gone loony, with adults taking a totally unrealistic view of what children are really like and how they really behave. Have you ever made a visit to the playground of your local primary school at break-time? I assure you it is one of the most violent places on earth!

Morris Minus and Polly Plus, however, were a different mat-ter. Again, the book caused a public outcry and, following pres-sure by the Working Group Against Racism, was not reprinted. Quite rightly, in my opinion. For Morris Minus was black and, as his name suggests, was 'minus' everything. And guess what? Polly Plus was white.

Both these books are now out of print. Other books, includ-ing 'classics' such as *Noddy*, have been rewritten to conform with current thinking. Again quite rightly. Some of Enid Blyton's characterisation leaves a very unpleasant taste in my mouth. Yet some people get all hot and bothered at the mere mention of political correctness. 'The trouble with children's books today,' writers complain, 'is that they have to be so terribly PC. Don't they?'

Or, 'I used to love fairy stories when I was a child. But they're not allowed these days, are they?' Or, 'I've given my book a "green" theme because I thought that would make it more PC.'

Let's examine those complaints. In my opinion, being politically correct means using a bit of common sense, being responsible. The only time you have deliberately to set out to write a politically correct book is when writing for the educational market, which has much more rigid requirements. Yet if, for example, we take the subject of schools, then books set in boarding schools will not have wide appeal – the large majority of the population could not afford to send their children to boarding school, even if they wanted to. Stories set in schools should, on the whole, be based in the state sector and must reflect a multi-cultural society – because that's the way it is.

On the other hand, beware of going too far. Just because we have equality of the sexes these days doesn't mean that you can *never* portray a woman washing up, or *never* portray a man mending a car. Children's writers have the freedom to create situations and form characters in whichever way they want – providing they reflect the situation of the population as a whole.

One of the problems with recreating traditional Fairy Tales for today's child is that Fairy Tales of the past haven't always been terribly politically correct. Before you all start groaning, here me out.

Most Fairy Tales are about boys, men and male adventures. When females do feature in the tales, they tend to play insignificant, passive roles, or are portrayed as evil, ugly schemers. Loving, watching, serving or hatching evil are the main activities permitted to women in Fairy Tales.

There is little doubt that children learn a great deal about the world through stories, so what does this highly popular form of the story say about the role of women? That girls are not very important or positive characters? That females have less exciting, less varied, less independent and less intelligent lives than males?

I'm not suggesting for one minute that you start producing stories such as those featured in James Finn Garner's wonderful collection of Politically Correct Bedtime Stories. These were written, tongue-in-cheek, to make a point *against* 'sexist, racist, sizeist, ethnocentrist reading matter'. Finn Garner's version of 'Little (Vertically Challenged surely!) Red Riding Hood' has the resolute young feminist setting off to her grandmother's house with a basket of fresh fruit and mineral water 'not because this is women's work, mind you, but because the deed was generous and helped to engender a feeling of community'.

As you can probably tell, Finn Garner's deeply ironic and sophisticated stories are written for adults. Nevertheless, the last twenty years has seen the traditional Fairy Tale turned upside down. Helpless princesses, wicked stepmothers and triumphant (male) wolves have been replaced by more positive role models, and less predictable outcomes.

As far as giving a 'green' theme, or any other sort of PC theme, to a children's book is concerned, do be very careful. Remember that the story must come first and that children will be highly sceptical of any message that is forced upon them rather than growing naturally from the story.

National Curriculum

This is another area which disturbs writers largely because they think that books must fit in with the National Curriculum and they haven't got a clue what that might involve.

So here goes: the programme of Study for Reading in the 1995 National Curriculum Orders states that 'the main emphasis should be on the encouragement of wider reading in order to develop independent, responsive and enthusiastic readers' and that children should read 'from a range of genres that includes stories, poetry, plays and picture books'.

Doesn't sound too arduous, does it? Certainly nothing to get in a state over. Yet authors can work themselves into a terrible sweat trying to find out what subject areas are being covered by the National Curriculum. If I've seen one novel about Vikings I've seen a hundred – and all because writers know that this subject is covered in schools and assume that, therefore, publishers will be desperate to publish fiction centred on that period of history.

Well, they have a point. But once one or two books (which are more than likely to be commissioned from authors they already know) have been published, the demand will have been satisfied. Forget the National Curriculum. In all likelihood the last thing children will want to do is read fiction based on a subject on which they've just completed a homework assignment.

Non-Fiction

I recently attended a meeting on non-fiction books for children entitled *The Very Bloody History of Non-Fiction (without the boring bits!)*. This was, in fact, a play on the title of John Farman's book, *The Very Bloody History of Britain Without the Boring Bits* (John was a speaker at the meeting), but the choice of meeting title makes a serious point about writing children's non-fiction – that fun and serious information go hand in hand.

Obviously non-fiction books are primarily there to educate, so any writer wanting to write for this market will have to consider the age group they are writing for when coming up with ideas. For the under five's, for example, as well as focusing on learning subjects such as counting, colours, shapes, time, etc., non-fiction books will also focus on 'situations' such as shopping, going to the park, etc. For this age group it is a question of giving a familiar subject a different angle.

One publisher (now sadly out of business) came up with a series of weather books. *My First Weather Books*, written by Hannah Roche and illustrated by Pierre Pratt, all feature the same characters and their friends set in the same familiar setting (a park). The books are, technically, an education into the four seasons for the under three's but, rather than focus directly on the seasons, the stories look at the weather as *experienced* by little children. Each book examines how different weather, happening at different times of the year, changes our surroundings. A slide in *Pete's Puddles* is slippery and wet during the rain, whereas in *Suki's Sun Hat* it is too hot to use.

For the older age group ideas are, to a certain extent, going to have to follow the dictates of the National Curriculum. But even here there is huge scope for flexibility. New writer Mary Dobson created a sensation with her first non-fiction books – *Smelly Old Histories*. These are 'scratch and sniff' books and give a real 'sense of the past' through smell. In *Tudor Odours*, for example, the reader can smell how Henry VIII's worn sock might have smelt – diseased toe and all! Other titles include *Victorian Vapours* and *Roman Aromas*.

One other thing to bear in mind when coming up with ideas for non-fiction books is that, like picture books, many non-fiction books are expensive to produce. They are often large format books and will usually require extensive colour artwork and/or colour photographs. If you can give your idea international appeal it will be much easier to sell your book in large quantities and, consequently, make it a more attractive proposition as far as publishers are concerned.

IDEAS AND INSPIRATION

In my experience writers tend to fall into two categories: those who have more ideas for stories than they know what to do with and yet can't put them down on paper, and those who find the writing part easy, yet are often struggling for inspiration.

Coming up with an idea is easy – it's just a question of turning every aspect of your day into a potential story. So take a deep breath and start by thinking what has happened to you so far today? Did the postman deliver a wrong letter to your address? Who was that woman who shook her fist at you as you crossed the road? And, this evening, did you really see lights in that boarded-up house next to the school?

Probably none of these things happened to you, but they are examples of everyday things which *could* have happened and could easily be turned into a book idea. Catherine MacPhail's inspiration for her first children's books came from a true, and terrible, event that happened to her daughter.

Catherine's daughter was being bullied at school and the bullying eventually culminated in her daughter being attacked by a gang of girls and dangled by her feet off a bridge over a busy road. The result of this incident was the writing of *Run Zan Run*, a book which went on to win the Kathleen Fidler Award. As Catherine herself has said, teasingly, to her daughter, 'It may be the worst thing that ever happened to you, pet – but it's the best thing that ever happened to me!'

If, like Catherine, you can get ideas from children themselves, you have the added advantage of knowing that what you have come up with is going to be of real interest. Another way of coming up with ideas is to scan newspapers and magazines. Newspapers and magazines can help focus the mind on what is 'real' for children today. For a children's book, I hear you murmur. Yes, for a children's book. For many a workshop session I have turned up laden with every conceivable tabloid newspaper and tacky magazine, which I have then thrown onto the floor, telling the group they have twenty minutes to come up with an idea. The results, often prompted by the most unlikely stories, have been quite spectacular. And Anne Fine's *Flour Babies* was prompted by her reading in the newspaper of a real-life experiment conducted in the States. A class of delinquent children had been given bags of flour to look after for a week and a prize went to the child who brought back their 'flour baby' in the best condition.

Another novel recently submitted to me was called *The Quiet Bride*. I found the title quite intriguing and was even more intrigued to find that the book was based on a true story that the author had found in the newspaper, *Orlando Sentinel*:

JILTED BRIDE WHO LIVED 35 YEARS IN GARDEN DIES
Reading, England – An English bride who lived in her garden for 35 years after being abandoned at the altar was found dead over the weekend. Joan Abery, 70, had refused to go back into her home after being spurned by her fiancé. She built herself a shelter from trees, twigs and brightly coloured umbrellas in the front garden of her home and furnished it with car seats and briefcases. She had left her house unchanged since the day the wedding should have taken place.

More about this clipping at the end of this chapter.

Another way of keeping in touch with what children want and enjoy is by watching children's television. Children's programming (on terrestrial TV) runs from around 3.30PM until 6PM (if you include *Neighbours*), Monday to Friday. This will give you a good selection of programmes for all age groups and is a couple of hours well spent; it will accurately illustrate current fashions, trends and interests. So pour yourself a mug of tea, put your feet up and indulge in a well-deserved break in front of the television. And if anyone asks, say I said it was okay!

And it goes without saying that you should think about the children's books you enjoy and consider what it was that inspired them. Often this will give you a clue as to where to hunt for your own inspiration.

Remembering Ideas

Once you've got those ideas flowing thick and fast, you have to learn how to remember them and translate them into workable fiction concepts.

How often have you woken in the night after the most amazing dream and thought, 'I'll definitely remember it in the morning – and then woken the next morning with no clearer recollection than a faint niggling feeling about nothing in particular at the back of your mind? The only way to remember that dream is to sit straight up and *write it down*.

It's the same with ideas. When you have one, *write it down*. Not in a few hours' time, or the next day, or even the next time you think of it. Write it down *immediately*. Get into the habit of always having a pen and paper handy, even when you go to bed.

Once you have written down your ideas you need to decide how you're going to store them. One solution is to have an 'ideas book' where you note down ideas as they come to you; sometimes, as already mentioned, ideas might come from a newspaper or magazine clipping, in which case it is better to cut out the item and keep it. I would suggest buying a box, or file, where you can keep both cuttings and the ideas book together. Review these regularly. If you're the highly organised type you could invest in a card index system and have all your ideas neatly categorised by subject; but remember that if you categorise an idea too rigidly at the start, you can inhibit its development later on.

Developing Ideas

Okay – you've got to the stage where you've had a few ideas and you've written them down. Now you need to start developing them. Sit down with your box or file and sift through the various thoughts you've had. Pick out one which really takes your fancy; different ideas will appeal at different times and there's no earthly point in struggling with an idea which you don't feel enthusiastic about – yet. And you're ready to try and develop it.

Now pose the question '*What if?*' This opens up all sorts of possibilities.

Take the wrongly delivered letter I mentioned previously.

What if you open it and discover that it contains a treasure map? *What if* it is a blackmail letter, not for you but for that nice boy who lives next door? *What if* it is addressed to someone who *used* to live next door but has long since been dead?

See what I mean? Already you have the beginnings of three different types of stories – an Adventure Story, a Thriller and a Ghost Story.

Another method is brainstorming – this can be done either on your own or in a group. Write down your initial story idea in the middle of the page and draw a circle around it. Then let your imagination run riot. So turn to page 102, let's take the word 'letter' and see where we get to.

I'll leave it up to you to come up with a story from the map above. Bear in mind that it doesn't have to be centred round the idea with which you started – you may well find that one of your 'offshoots' provides you with most inspiration.

Ideas: Exercises

- Write a story based on the newspaper clipping from the *Orlando Sentinel*.
- Buy a tabloid newspaper and, after scanning its pages, develop a story idea from something you have read or seen in it.
- Apply the question 'what if?' to the initial idea and see what happens.

CHAPTER ELEVEN

PLOTTING

Some writers say that they have no idea what is going to happen in their story until they write it.

'A book just *happens*, doesn't it? I just go with the flow.'

While I wouldn't want to discourage such spontaneity, unless they are very experienced writers indeed they will often end up with a seemingly unconnected series of events with no discernible beginning, middle or end, and no structure on which to base the other aspects of their story.

A book needs to be planned very carefully before the actual process of writing begins. This doesn't mean that change isn't possible once you have started to write. After all, half the fun of writing fiction is that characters become so real that they get up and speak and act for themselves. However, if you at least set off with some form of 'map', then you know where to take the detours and, most importantly, when to return to the main route once more.

In his book *Writing for Children and Teenagers*, Lee Wyndham describes plot as 'a plan of action devised to achieve a definite and much desired end – through cause and effect'. I would perhaps have added 'theme' to that list.

THEME

Theme can be differentiated from Subject Matter by thinking of it as the message behind your book. Say, for example, you've chosen to write about the subject of homelessness – what message do you want to convey? Do you want to say that homeless people are helpless victims; that they are just the same as ordinary people, except they have nowhere to live; that society is responsible for homelessness? The theme should evolve naturally from the bare bones of your story – if you focus on it too obviously, you will be in danger of becoming didactic. Often the real theme of your book will only reveal itself when you have finished writing – that isn't a problem. So long as some sort of basic truth is illustrated by the end of the book, you have theme enough.

CAUSE

Cause is the whole *point* of your book. It is what makes your main character take action to solve a problem or reach a certain goal.

The chapter headings in *Winnie the Pooh* are good examples of cause – 'In Which Eeyore Loses a Tail . . .' 'In Which Piglet Meets a Hefalump . . .', 'In Which Pooh Is Completely Surrounded By Water . . .'

If you are unsure about the cause of your story ask yourself one simple question, 'What is my story *about*?' Don't answer this question in terms of theme – i.e. it is about love/jealousy/revenge – answer it, instead, in factual terms. Narrow down your answer to one sentence and, hopefully, you will have it – your cause.

Author Malorie Blackman's book *That New Dress* opens:

Wendy was sad.
  Wendy was mad.
  'Grandma, I haven't got a dress to wear to Jennifer's party tomorrow,' Wendy said.

There you have it, in the first few sentences of the book – the *cause*, the thing that is going to make this book 'happen'. Wendy is going to a party the next day and she has nothing to wear. *That* basically, is what this book is all about.

It is interesting to note how quickly this author has established the cause. This is particularly important when writing for younger children. The longer and more ambitious the book, the more time the author has to get to the point. In picture books the cause should be clearly established within the first few lines; in shorter chapter books by the end of the first chapter; in longer chapter books by the end of the first two or three chapters – at the latest! By this time we must know what the book is going to be *about* – not what is going to happen, but what it is about.

Another important point to bear in mind is that the cause must be *crucial* to the main character. The fact that Wendy doesn't have a dress to wear to Jennifer's party isn't a matter of life and death – but it is desperately important to Wendy. And because it is important to the central character, it is important to the reader. We are going to read this book because we want to know how things turn out for the character with whom we most identify.

The cause is complicated by the fact that Wendy has set her heart on a new dress from Mr MacKenzie's shop window and nothing else will do. Unfortunately her mother has set her heart on making Wendy a dress and the new dress is absolutely out of the question. Here you start to see the effect of the cause and a series of events is set up which *prevents* the central character from achieving her heart's desire.

And this is the Plot. The Cause has to be resolved by the end of the book. In *That New Dress* Wendy arrives at the party:

> Hey! that was funny. Wow! that was odd. All the girls at the party were like peas in a pod. They each wore the dress that she'd wanted to wear. So hers was the only different dress there.

The end of the book refers directly back to the original cause. In chapter books almost every chapter needs to do this. There is nothing more irritating for the reader than establishing a cause and then wandering so far away from it that all cohesiveness is lost and resolution becomes impossible.

EFFECT

As already mentioned, effect is what happens as a result of cause. It can also be described as a series of connected events preventing the cause from being resolved.

If, in *That New Dress*, Wendy had nothing to wear for a party (cause) and then, on the very next page, found a dress to wear (effect), there would be no story.

Obviously this is not what happens. Instead, Wendy goes from family member to family member, bemoaning the fact that she has nothing to wear, letting them know how desperately she wants one of the dresses Mr MacKenzie is selling. She even visits Mr MacKenzie's shop where he offers to save her one of the dresses if her family will let her buy one. Slowly the chain of events is built up and we see and feel and understand Wendy's longing (another effect).

In this way suspense is intertwined with reader involvement. Because of this series of events, and the way that Wendy is portrayed, the reader is as keen as Wendy that she should have that dress. Yet in our heart of hearts the reader knows, as does Wendy, that life isn't that simple. The cause *will* be resolved – but not in quite the way you might expect. It is important that effect isn't too predictable, and that sufficient conflict is introduced.

In *Jimmy Woods and the Big Bad Wolf* by Mick Gowar, the cause is established by the end of the first chapter: a bully, Jimmy Woods, is terrorising a community of children. We know that the bully will be defeated – it is *how* this is achieved (effect) that creates the dramatic tension. If the bully were to be defeated in Chapter Two, we would have no need to read the rest of the book.

THE MECHANICS OF PLOTTING

Once you have decided on your cause and, in general terms, its effect, you can plot out your book.

A good plotting exercise is to think of an idea for a book of around 3000 words. Divide those words into ten chapters and roughly plot out what is going to happen in each. This way you get the balance of your book right.

For example, the plot outline for *Jimmy Woods and the Big Bad Wolf* may have looked like this:

1 Jimmy Woods picks on hero as he makes his way to sweet shop. Steals his sweet money.

2 Hero takes his dog, Prince, to the shops and Prince scares off a terrified Jimmy Woods – for now.

3 Jimmy Woods is spotted by hero paying a visit to Granny Timpson's house. Hero is worried and decides to check up on Granny Timpson.

4 Granny Timpson won't let Hero into her house. Hero's sister, Debbie, persuades her to let her in.

5 Hero is allowed in as well. Discovers that Jimmy Woods is terrorising Granny Timpson and stealing from her.

6 Hero and Debbie put a plan into action. Involves sitting Prince in chair in dark room with rug over him to make him look like Granny. Prince goes for Jimmy Woods and chases him off – for good this time.

7 Story of how Jimmy Woods was scared off by a 'wolf' gets around but no-one believes him. He is laughing stock and no longer a threat.

Every chapter is relevant to, and advances, the main cause. It inevitably works its way towards resolution, but the cause and tension is maintained by constantly introducing new elements to the story.

The story itself, though, is worked through logically, with approximately two 'events' in each chapter, and neither 'accident' nor 'coincidence' play any part in the plotting plan. This helps sustain the credibility of the story. If you are tempted (or forced!) to use coincidence as a way of resolving your story, look again at the plot – it is usually a sign of weakness on the writer's part.

Note, also, that factual happenings only have been used in the plotting plan. This is crucial. Many other details will, of course, be included in this story as it progresses, but it is worth remembering that character analysis and background detail are not 'plot'. In children's fiction they make the plot seem more interesting; they do not in themselves advance the story.

Catherine's Plan

Catherine MacPhail won the (then) Kathleen Fidler Award with her book *Run Zan Run*. She uses her own special formula for plotting out her books which, with her permission, I am now going to share with you.

She begins by working out, roughly, how many chapters she is going to have in her book. *Run Zan Run* is between 20–25,000 words; Catherine would have known that it was going to be roughly this length before she started writing because it is specified in the Award rules. So, once she had her idea, she decided that sixteen chapters was going to be a feasible length, ensuring chapters were neither too long nor too short.

She then writes down the following headings:

1 *What is the problem?*
2 *Build on the problem?*
3 *Open out the plot . . .*

4–12 *Filler*

13 *Crescendo*
14 *Nothing Can Save Her Now!*
15 *Baddies get done in*
16 *Tidy up*

Let's run through this plan and see how it applied to *Run Zan Run*, the book Catherine ended up writing.

What is the Problem?

Katie is being mercilessly bullied by Ivy Toner and her cronies:

> Everyone told her one day Ivy Toner would grow tired of picking on her, move on to fresher, more fearing ground.
> But when? It had been months since it began . . .

This is the problem. It is what the book is about. Katie is being bullied by a gang of girls to such an extent that the reader feels they could even threaten her life. Obviously it is *crucial* to Katie that this problem – this cause – is resolved. And if it is crucial to Katie, it is crucial to the reader.

Build on the Problem

Once the basic problem has been set up, we need to explore it in more detail.

By the end of Chapter 1 Zan, the mysterious girl who lives in a cardboard box on the dump, has been introduced. In Chapter 2 her role becomes more important as we see her starting to befriend Katie and side with her against the evil Ivy:

> The girl stepped from the darkness. Zan. Her face dirty and her hair matted, but her eyes bright and challenging.
> 'You again . . .' Ivy's voice trembled. She was afraid. Ivy Toner was afraid!

Some background detail is also built into this chapter – not in one big chunk but gradually as, piece by piece, we learn the finer details of Katie's life. Such as what her parents are like and her relationship with them:

> 'Is something bothering you, Katie?' Her mother sat across from her. She was very pretty with large dark eyes and a head of rich dark curls. She looked much younger than her forty-four years.

Or details about where Katie lives:

> Zan held back, looking at the house. How inviting it must seem to her, Katie thought. The warm glow of the lamps lighting the windows, the hall lit up and the red carpeted stairs rising to the floor above. There were sounds too, music and laughter. Her parents' party in full progress. Katie wanted her to come in so much.

Opening up the Plot

Obviously the fact that Katie is being bullied isn't alone sufficient to sustain a book of this length. Other factors need to be developed to give the plot depth and interest.

This added depth is provided by Zan, who is appalled at the fact that Katie has told everyone about her:

> 'They're everywhere,' Zan went on breathlessly. 'Police, social workers, do-gooders. I wanted to stay here for a while. I like this town, it's big enough to hide in, but not

to get lost in . . . Now I can't – because of you – I helped you. I've never helped anyone in my life . . . and this is how you thank me.'

Katie is forced into a position of having to lie about Zan. She tells everyone that she made her up and everyone believes her, even Ivy's two cronies. Their own theory about Zan is that she was really Katie in disguise. Everyone believes Katie – except for Ivy, and Ivy is going to prove that Zan exists even if it takes to the end of her days.

Filler

The middle part of the book contains the bulk of the plot – the effect – what Catherine MacPhail calls the *Filler*.

It's hard to be specific about exactly how *you* should fill your book without knowing the specific story you want to write. Read *Run Zan Run* to see how Catherine did it. Think about how your baddie prevents your hero from resolving the initial problem; consider what actions your hero takes to overcome these obstacles. One difficulty should constantly lead to another right the way through until the resolution.

Ask yourself the following as you finish each and every chapter: 'Has this chapter, in some way, addressed the initial problem – the cause – established in Chapter 1?' Be honest with yourself – if your text has strayed from the main route there is a danger that your reader will get lost.

Crescendo

Towards the end of the book, there should be a 'plateau of awfulness'. This is where the tension builds and everything that *can* go wrong *does* go wrong. Various strands of the plot begin to be pulled together, but resolution still seems as far away as ever.

In *Run Zan Run* this point comes in Chapter 13 when we discover Zan's terrible secret – the reason why her existence must never be discovered. She believes she is suspected of causing a fire in her parent's home in which they both died. We learn who the real killer is as the plot reaches its crescendo:

'I saw him, Katie . . . the man who did burn the house down. And he saw me. He said he'd get me one day . . . I've been running ever since.'

Nothing Can Save Her Now!

Just as we think nothing can get any worse the plot spirals out of control into a final 'black' moment. In *Run Zan Run* the killer has cornered Zan and Ivy Toner finally gets Katie on her own, without Zan to help her.

> No one knew where she was. No one knew Zan existed. It was hopeless praying for help. Nothing could save her now!

Baddies Get Done In

In all children's books 'good' somehow has to triumph over 'bad'. This won't necessarily mean that the 'baddies get done in', but it will mean that the 'goodies' come out on top.

In *Run Zan Run* the cavalry arrive at the last minute in the shape of Katie's teacher, her Mum and Dad, and two policeman. Katie is rescued from Ivy, and Zan from the killer. The truth dawns and everyone sees Ivy for what she really is – a stupid, but nonetheless evil, bully.

Tidying Up

The last chapter is there to tidy up any loose ends. It should be brief and to the point. If you do feel a need to go on at length it may mean you have a weak link in your plot, an aspect which has not been resolved as a consequence of events. This final chapter should also underline the 'basic truth' of your book – the theme, or message.

Catherine's final chapter is barely four pages, yet it tells us everything we need to know:

> 'I'd like to propose a toast,' her father said, and he held his glass high. 'To Katie and Zan . . .' He smiled at each of them. 'Friends for ever.'

Plotting: Exercises

- Choose a children's book that you like (not a Picture Book or very young Reader) and work out the plot outline chapter by chapter.

- Think of a book idea of your own, sum up what it is *about* and try to narrow this down to one sentence.
- Take Catherine's Plan and work out how it could apply to your own book.

Obviously your own personal plan may vary a little according to the sort of book you are writing. But if you adapt the bare bones of Catherine's plan to your needs you won't go far wrong, whoever you are writing for.

CHAPTER TWELVE

CHARACTERISATION

Characterisation makes your story come alive. However strong your plot, without good characterisation you will have an uninvolving, superficial text on your hands: at best boring, at worst, dead.

Take those classics of children's literature, *Winnie the Pooh* and *The House at Pooh Corner*. They don't have the most exciting plots in the world. But combined with exquisitely drawn characters the story becomes compulsive reading for young and old alike.

ANIMAL CHARACTERS

One of the reasons A.A. Milne's characters are so brilliant is that their individual characteristics are entirely human. As a group, the characters in *Pooh* form a typical community in which any one of us might live. There's an Eeyore in every street – the gloomy pessimist, always looking on the dark side. And a happy-go-lucky Pooh, who 'hasn't much brain but never comes to any harm'. And an Owl, who 'hasn't exactly got a brain, but he Knows Things'. And a scheming Rabbit, who 'hasn't learnt in books but can always think of a Clever Plan'.

A.A. Milne's writing demonstrates that, even when we're writing about animals, characterisation is every bit as important as it is when we're writing about human beings. I once attended a children's writing workshop and one of the students was writing a story about a cat – but the story wasn't working because none of us really *believed* in the cat. Then someone suggested that the cat reminded him of the woman who does the wine slot on a food and drink television programme (I name no names!). By the time of the next workshop session the writer concerned had incorporated the woman's very specific characterisations into her cat. The cat sprang to life in front of our eyes – or ears! She became real: we could see her, hear her, feel her, almost touch her.

So if you are having trouble with your animal characters – if you feel that you have just another squirrel on your hands, or just another rabbit – base them on someone you know. The character will then become real in your mind and, as a result, real to your reader.

HUMAN CHARACTERS

Human characters often present more problems. Many writers find that, whilst they are clear about their less detailed subsidiary characters, their main character refuses to develop beyond a one-dimensional cardboard cut-out. I think this is because our main character is often ourselves; it is the character we can identify with, the one from whose viewpoint the story is told. And, as in life, we can see the people around us by looking outwards, but to see ourselves we need a mirror.

For this reason many writers find it helpful to develop their main character while studying a photograph or drawing. Don't feel ashamed about this; it doesn't mean that you have no imagination, it just means that you are identifying with your main character to such an extent that it is impossible to be completely objective.

As I said earlier, a character can sometimes be created by a newspaper or magazine feature, or photograph. In my files I have a large newspaper photograph of a young teenager sitting in the driving seat of a car, with a cigarette hanging out of his mouth and a black woolly cap pulled down over a white, pinched face. One day I will write about that boy – and I will need that picture to keep him alive.

School photographs can be useful. All those rows and rows of children staring at the camera – that one, third from the right in the second row – he's got a look about him. What was he like? Why is the boy next but one to him glancing across at him?

When I was working for teenage magazines, we used to employ young models and actors to act out the photostories. The writers all kept details of these young people, including their photographs. These proved vital when coming up with new storylines on a weekly basis; often a photograph alone would be enough to spark off an idea.

However, it would be a mistake to think that the best way of conveying a character, any character, is by describing them in photographic detail. Sometimes a better impression of a character can be given by focusing on just one part of their body, or dress or on something that they do, or are doing. Take this passage from *Junk* by Melvin Burgess where we meet Lily for the first time:

> She was dancing. I mean she was doing things and dancing at the same time. She'd go and put on a new cassette, or find a better track on the old one or just look through what was there, then she'd go over and pinch a fag or a joint off someone, or tidy up fag ends or paper cups or something . . . and all the time she was moving to the music, dancing, swaying her head, just really going with the music. She just couldn't stand still. She was smiling all the time, not at anyone, just to herself and the good time she was having. Her mouth was even wider than mine and her eyes turned into two, black, happy little gaps in her face when she smiled. She was beautiful.

By the end of this passage we know nothing about the way Lily looks except that she has a wide mouth and black eyes. Yet I can see her . . . and I *know*, without knowing anything else about her, that she *is* beautiful.

But it isn't just the look of someone that brings a character to life. Smell, sound, feel, likes and dislikes are all part of a person as well. Have you noticed, for example, how often characters in children's fiction are portrayed as liking a particular food? Popeye was mad about spinach; Paddington Bear's staple diet was marmalade just as Pooh's was honey; the Teenage Mutant Hero Turtles loved pizza.

Children's author Philip Ridley, knows this better than anyone. In his book *Krindlekrax* Ruskin's mum can't live without teabags and toast. In *Kasper in the Glitter* Kasper is an expert at making Banoffi pie because he knows that it cheers his mum up:

Banoffi is one of the most delicious pies ever invented. It's made with sliced bananas, gooey toffee, and topped off with coffee-flavoured cream, chocolate granules, and a large dollop of marmalade.

The marmalade, to be honest, is Kasper's own particular addition to the recipe. He says it gives the dish a much-needed twang. And he should know. After all, nobody could have made as many Banoffi pies as ten-year-old Kasper Whisky.

Note the detail that Philip gives to this description. He gets right inside Kasper's head by describing something as inconsequential as how to make a Banoffi pie. Food is something all of us can relate to – it elicits an immediate emotional response in adults and children alike.

Philip Ridley also uses nicknames to reinforce his characters. In *The Meteorite Spoon* Filly and Fergal call each other Sis and Brov; in *Krindlekrax* the school caretaker is called Corky. This happens in real life, so why not in books? It's yet another technique to make your characters seem more tangible, more real – more like the child reading about them.

So before sitting down to write your story I suggest that you write a complete separate profile of your main character, for your reference only. Think about the foods that your character likes; hobbies; friends; what he or she sounds like; smells like; the look of the skin on his face; how often she has to wash her hair – *everything*, and *anything*, you can think of. I once asked some students to think of a person they knew and write down two things which best summed them up. One lady was a teacher and the character she wrote about was a boy in her class. The two characteristics she assigned him were 'squelchy armpits' and 'the smell of plasticine'. I never met him, but I can see that child to this day!

One final tip (for the very lazy) on bringing your main character to life; buy a book on star signs. I have a wonderful book called *Heaven on Earth* by Fritz Wegner: it certainly isn't a book for the astrological expert, but for my purposes it is unrivalled.

Let's take a fictional character, Lucy, born on 25th March. My book immediately tells me she's an Arian, which is the sign of the ram. It also tells me that her likes are 'anything new, fast, fun, thrilling or competitive'. In action she is 'swift and intrepid. Has a direct manner and clear-cut views; remarks are candid and often satirical. Is determined, and does not take kindly to being thwarted'. At best she is 'enthusiastic, courageous, carefree, amicable, exciting, decisive, straightforward, quick-witted and energetic'. At worst she is 'headstrong, irresponsible, vain, hot-tempered, aggressive, ruthless, reckless, tactless and egotistical'.

It tells me a whole host of other things as well, including her favourite gemstones, the sort of people she gets on with and what she's like at school. Maybe Fritz Wegner should write a children's book . . .

SUBSIDIARY CHARACTERS

Don't forget that your main character isn't the only character in your book. Subsidiary characters can be just as important to the story, but too often they come across as nothing more than shadows.

The number of characters you should include in your story depends upon the length of the book and, therefore, the age group you are writing for. Generally speaking the younger the age group, and the shorter the book, the fewer characters you should have. In many picture books there are often only one or two characters. *Rosie's Walk* by Pat Hutchins has a hen and a fox: *Winnie the Witch* by Valerie Thomas and Korky Paul, a witch and her cat. This is because, in picture books, situations are as important as the characters and simplicity is vital. But the older the age group, the more important the characters become, and the more characters and complexity you will need to include.

Subsidiary characters often provide the opportunity for a subplot. In a very serious story they can provide opportunities for light relief. They are also good 'sounding boards' for the main character – through conversations with a subsidiary character the reader can learn how the main character is really feeling.

Remember, too, that no one character exists in isolation from another. The way that characters interact with each other tell us more about them, as people, than anything that they do. Body language can be just as telling as words.

Take this following passage from *Stone Cold* by Robert Swindells:

> She came over. Every eye in the place followed her. She nodded at one of the three empty chairs. 'Anyone sitting here?' She sounded Scottish. I shook my head.
>
> 'Mind if I join you then?' I nodded, saying nothing. Being the New Me. She unslung her pack, dropped it next to mine and sat down. I lifted my mug and sipped tepid coffee, gazing out of the window.
>
> She inserted her straw in her Coke and sucked. When I risked a glance at her she dropped her eyes. I sipped more coffee, sensing her eyes on my face. I mean I could actually feel them, like lasers.

The attraction between the two is almost palpable. It is far more intense than if the author had written about her falling into his arms. This is how young people *really* behave when they fancy each other. They size each other up, glance at each other and then look away, feel self-conscious, act cool. We've all been there so use your experiences.

Stereotyping

There is a danger, when coming up with characters for a story, of falling into the trap of stereotyping: your baddie is unshaven and wearing a dirty raincoat, even though you know perfectly well that the most dangerous psychopaths are immaculately dressed and baby-faced; Granny is grey-haired and sitting in a rocking chair knitting booties, even though your own granny dresses in leathers and rides a motorbike.

Try, whenever possible, to turn the expected into the unexpected. Think of the stereotype – then write about the opposite. Many popular stories are based around role reversal – Kaye

Umansky's *Romantic Giant*, whose title speaks for itself; Dick King-Smith's *The Sheep-Pig*, the story of a pig who think he's a sheep; *The Three Little Wolves and the Big Bad Pig* by Eugene Trivizas and Helen Oxenbury; and *Clever Polly and the Stupid Wolf* by Catherine Storr.

One of my favourites is *Crummy Mummy and Me* by Anne Fine. This is a collection of stories about an outrageously irresponsible Mum, her slightly more responsible punk boyfriend, and Mum's ever-sensible and practical daughter, Mina. The following passage is a conversation between Mum and Mina at bedtime:

MINA: I really think I ought to be going up to bed now.
MUM: (*astonished*) Why?
MINA: (*patiently*) Because it's getting rather late.
MUM: It's not *that* late.
MINA: (*looking at her watch*) It's well past my bedtime.
MUM: Oh, you're getting older all the time. You don't need that much sleep.
MINA: I do. Look at me. I've already got great big grey bags under my eyes.
MUM: That's just the light.
MINA: No it isn't.
MUM: Well, what about this board game? Surely you can stay long enough to finish the *game*? It's nearly over.
MINA: It's nowhere near over. It'll take *ages*.
MUM: Oh, all *right*. Go on, then. I'll come up in a little while and tuck you in.
MINA: (*really relieved*) Oh, good, Mum. Thanks.

Role reversal at its best and funniest. And this passage brings me neatly on to the final, and most important, element of characterisation – dialogue.

DIALOGUE AND CHARACTERISATION

You can tell a lot about a person from the way that they speak. A shy person may stammer on certain words; someone who is not very sure of themselves may speak in short, unfinished sentences.

A very confident person may constantly interrupt, cutting other people short.

In Philip Ridley's *Krindlekrax* Ruskin Bond's mum, Wendy, says 'Polly-wolly-doodle-all-the-day' whenever she gets flustered. Ruskin's Dad, on the other hand, is always saying, 'It's not my fault.' Both these phrases, when used in dialogue, convey the characters of the users far better than any detailed description of the way they look and how they behave.

When writing dialogue it is important to *sum up* the character of the particular person you are writing about and style their speech accordingly. The reader should be able to tell who is speaking without being told – *just* from the way the dialogue is written.

Take this dialogue from *The House at Pooh Corner*.

'I don't know how it is, Christopher Robin, but what with all this snow and one thing and another, not to mention icicles and such-like, it isn't so Hot in my field about three o'clock in the morning as some people think it is. It isn't Close, if you know what I mean – not so as to be uncomfortable. It isn't Stuffy. In fact, Christopher Robin' he went on in a loud whisper, 'quite-between-ourselves-and-don't-tell-anybody, it's Cold.'

It's Eeyore speaking. It couldn't be anyone else – his dialogue *sums up* everything we know about him: his lugubriousness, his pessimism.

Dialect is another factor to consider when writing dialogue. The trick is to convey an accent, complete with all its mannerisms and oddities, while making it intelligible.

The following examples are from *Run Zan Run* by Cathy MacPhail:

'There's no' anywhere you can hide here, hen.'
'You gonny make me?'
'She fairly scared the knickers off you anyway.'
'You jist tell her to stay away from me.'

Note the words Cathy uses – *hen, gonny, jist* – all characteristic of the Scottish idiom. She thus helps to establish not only the background of her characters, but also a strong sense of place. And for the reader, the unfamiliar yet recognisable words provide a rich and colourful reading experience.

The way your character speaks must fit in with the type of book that you are writing. Just as if a story is set in Scotland you must convey a Scottish accent, so if a story is set in the past your dialogue must give a flavour of those times. For this reason, if you don't feel confident about writing dialogue, make sure that you set your story in a time and region familiar to you.

Even so it is vital that your dialogue is realistic, so do listen to how people speak – and, in particular, how children speak: how they speak *today*, not how they spoke when you were a child.

'Children swear a lot today. Is it all right to have swearing in my book?' is a question I often get asked. It's hard to answer this one. Gratuitous swearing is not allowed but swearing that fits with the style of your story is acceptable in fiction for teenagers. My advice would be to cut out swearing altogether except where absolutely necessary and don't ever use the 'stronger' swear words. And if you *are* using swear words, or any form of slang, do make sure that the words you use are up-to-date. At the time of writing the word *cool* has come in, gone out and come in again. In the 1990s many children use/have used unexpected adjectives such as *wizard* and *bad* to bestow praise – but these have now fallen from favour. It's impossible to stay ahead of the fashion, so try to keep your dialogue as timeless as possible.

We'll talk more about dialogue in the following two chapters: how to write it, how to use it to move the plot forward and how to achieve the correct balance of dialogue and narrative.

CHARACTER DEVELOPMENT

'Character Development' means just that – the characters in your book have to develop. If your main character is weak and silly at the beginning of your story and is still weak and silly at the end, what was the point of us reading your book. 'For the plot', I hear you say. 'To find out what happened.' Fine, but to read a book for plot alone isn't enough. Your characters have to move with the plot, they have to be affected in some way by the plot, and, as a result of what happens in the plot, they have to have changed in some way by the end – for better, or just occasionally in the case of subsiduary characters, for worse.

This is, after all, what happens in real life. The way in which we react to different situations determines who we are as people. Whether child or adult we don't stand still. Depending upon what happens to us we develop, we learn, we move on – that process is happening every day and it never stops. In the same way characters that we create in fiction have to learn from the situations in which they are placed.

In Anne Fine's *Flour Babies* Simon Martin learns that he isn't trapped in some sort of predestined downward spiral but is free to make his own decisions.

Louder and louder he sang. He wasn't trapped. He would be punished, but he wasn't trapped. And there'd be time enough to be responsible.

In Catherine MacPhail's *Run Zan Run* Katie and Zan learn to trust other people and learn the truth of the saying 'united we stand' first hand.

Her mother joined in hugging Zan too, and Katie, never one to be left out, just held on tight. She could feel Zan shaking, the fear still upon her, and she could feel that fear abate, as her father's strength, her family's strength, comforted her.

Even Robert Swindells' *Stone Cold*, which can hardly be said to have a happy ending, ends on a positive note. Talking about homelessness the main character writes:

There has to be an end to this. I just hope it happens while I'm still around.

But perhaps the most dramatic illustration of character development is to be found in *Junk* by Melvin Burgess. This is, essentially, a love story, but it is also a shocking portrayal of drug abuse and the degradation of the human spirit. The book has a wide cast of characters all of whom develop continually throughout the story. The two main characters, Tar and Gemma, learn something positive from their experience but this is far from the case for all of the characters involved in the story. For example this next extract is the last we hear from Tar's Dad.

> One day, my boy, all this will be yours. As they say. All my goods and shackles, such as they are. There's no one else. The other thing you leave your children is your life – the example of it. One day, my boy . . .
>
> And so, in your absense David, I raise my glass to you – a cup of tea actually – and I say, Here's to you. Good luck! Make the most of it.
>
> And don't end up like me.

Junk also teaches us a lot about creating characters with whom, although not necessarily sympathetic or likeable, we can identify. This is important. If a character is downright unpleasant from start to finish we won't want to read about him or her. Gemma in *Junk* is a far from likeable character yet, despite everything, we can identify with her, we can sympathise with her, we care about her. This is because she has two sides to her – she is strong and assertive, but she is also weak and vulnerable. It is a question of creating rounded characters. No-one is all bad, or all good; people are a mixture of the two, usually weighted one way or the other. That is how your characters should be in your book – real, rounded people, not just cardboard cut-outs.

Characterisation: Exercises

- Find an old school photo and, choosing a person you do like, and a person you don't like, list three small things which sum up each person.
- Bearing in mind the excerpt from *Crummy Mummy and Me* invent a dialogue between two people trying to get across their individual characteristics in the way that they speak.

CHAPTER THIRTEEN

VIEWPOINT

Viewpoint is the *position* from which a story is told. It is rather like the camera position chosen by a film director and, as the director, you the writer have two decisions to make before you start filming. One is to decide *which* viewpoint you are using; the other is to decide *whose*.

WHOSE VIEWPOINT?

When writing for children the main viewpoint character usually has to be a child. There are exceptions to this rule, particularly in books for younger children, but, even then, the viewpoint character is usually a child 'substitute' – ie. to all intents and purposes he or she *is* a child in an adult body. For example, *The Romantic Giant* by Kaye Umansky doesn't contain any child characters; the main viewpoint character is Waldo the giant. However, Waldo possesses an innocence and naivety which children are able to relate to.

It is the same with animal characters. Even if your main viewpoint character is not, technically, a young 'child' animal, he or she must possess qualities to which a child can relate. It is the quality of innocence which matters. I don't know what age Pooh is; or Mole in *The Wind in the Willows*. They are, in many ways, ageless. Both characters sometimes seem very old and wise, yet at other times they seem childlike and innocent. It is the innocence which appeals to the reading child.

Your viewpoint character must also be the same age, or preferably slightly older, than your target reader. Children like to feel 'grown-up' when they are reading and think it is 'babyish' to read about someone younger than they are. They want to be a little older, more mature, more powerful, than they are in reality – just as adults like to read about characters who are an idealised version of themselves. So if your book is targeted at the 8–12 age range, your viewpoint character ideally needs to be twelve plus. If it is a book essentially for the younger end of that age span, then twelve is fine. If it is really a story more suited to the older end then you will probably have to add a couple of years; for example, Katie, in *Run Zan Run*, is nearly fourteen. You don't need, necessarily, to be specific about the age of your viewpoint character; but you do need to think carefully about what stage of maturity your character has reached, so that you are clear about his or her experience and capabilities. It is no good writing a book for very young children which shows your viewpoint character walking to school on their own, or being at home on their own. Similarly, if you are writing a school story you need to think about the level that your viewpoint character has reached. Are they at primary school? If so, is it upper or lower, junior or 'middle'? Or have they moved on to secondary school?

When you've decided upon your viewpoint character's approximate age, draw up a 'plan' taking all aspects of their life into account: where they live, how they dress, what they eat, what music they listen to and so on. You need to inhabit that character's viewpoint before you can write about it.

WHICH VIEWPOINT?

In modern children's books the story is usually told through the eyes (and other senses) of one 'viewpoint character'. Up to a dozen different types of viewpoint are available to the children's writer but, in practice, only a few are regularly used. Let's run through the four basic choices with examples.

First Person
A story written in the first person is told from the point of view of the narrator. This person is the character the reader is going to identify with and appears as 'I' in the text.

It all began last January, on a dark evening that was full of
sleet. Funny, it's not long ago. I was just a kid then. But
today is October 2nd, and this is where I begin to write,
where I open a door into the past.

(From *Dear Nobody* by Berlie Doherty)

At first glance it would seem that this is an easy viewpoint choice
to handle. No problems with making the main character come
alive – because we are, straight away, inside the main character's
head.

However, first person does have its drawbacks. It is an introspective style of writing and doesn't really work when there is a
lot of action involved. Also, unless skilfully handled, it can
become monotonous.

Generally speaking it is a better choice when writing for older
children and teenagers, as this type of story tends to rely more on
introspection in any case.

Third Person Singular

This is the most popular viewpoint when writing for children.
In my opinion, it is the easiest to handle and the most effective.
The story is told in the third person (he, she or it) but from a
single point of view only.

Nothing can be described which is not *directly experienced* by
your viewpoint character. It is as if you, the writer, are sitting on
his or her shoulder and seeing events from there *only*. You can
know what your viewpoint character is feeling, but can only sur-
mise what other characters are feeling from the way they look,
behave and talk.

He climbed the stairs very slowly though, partly because he
was tired and partly because they'd started discussing the
Snells more seriously. His mother wasn't really amused any
more; perhaps all that silly tittering had been for his benefit. Eunice had been in such an awful state, waving those
hedgehogs, any child would have been unnerved by it.

'She's a bit obsessional,' he heard her telling Noreen.

(From *Henry's Leg* by Ann Pilling)

Note the phrase 'he heard her telling' – we, the reader, hear Mum speaking *through the ears of Henry*.

This viewpoint choice gives you all the advantages of strong reader identification with your main character, yet still leaves plenty of opportunity for descriptive narrative.

Third Person Plural or Multiple Viewpoint

This is where the story is told from no one particular viewpoint – the viewpoint shifts from person to person. Personally I don't think this is a choice any new writer should be considering, although a number of established children's authors do use multiple viewpoint. It does give a certain amount of flexibility, in that it is easy to move from location to location, but it certainly doesn't help reader identification.

Enid Blyton used this viewpoint very successfully, but her books were largely plot-led with very little time spent exploring the emotions of her characters. A more recent notable example of multiple viewpoint is *Madame Doubtfire* by Anne Fine:

> All the way up the stairs, the children fought not to carry the envelope. Towards the top, Lydia took advantage of her height to force it down Christopher's jumper. Christopher pulled it out and tried to thrust it into Natalie's hand.
> 'Here, Natty,' he said. 'Give this to Dad.'
> Natalie shook her head so violently her hair whipped her cheeks pink. She interlaced her fingers behind her back. So Christopher tucked the envelope down the top of her pinafore dress, behind the yellow felt ducklings. Natalie's eyes filled with tears, and by the time Daniel Hilliard opened the door to let his children in, she was weeping gently.

It is as if all the characters are being observed equally minutely by an all-knowing outsider looking down on them. This is multiple viewpoint.

Narrator Viewpoint

The most famous example of this type of viewpoint is the *Just So Stories* by Rudyard Kipling, where the author breaks away from his story to acknowledge his reader as 'Dearly Beloved'. A. A. Milne opens *Winnie the Pooh* using narrator viewpoint, as does C. S. Lewis in *The Chronicles of Narnia*:

> This is the story of something that happened long ago when your grandfather was a child. It is a very important story because it shows how all the comings and goings between our world and the land of Narnia first began.

This is a traditional, formal storytelling technique which isn't often used nowadays as it can sound rather studied and old-fashioned.

HOW TO CHOOSE

Sometimes it is obvious, even before the planning stage, which viewpoint type you are going to have to use for your story. It depends what sort of story you have decided to write. At other times, however, you may be faced with a dilemma.

The most common confusion usually arises over whether to use first person or third person singular. There is no easy answer. Sometimes it helps to start writing and discover for yourself which viewpoint comes most naturally to you.

Don't forget, though, that third person singular can be remarkably close to first person – particularly if you give voice to your main character's thoughts. When I was thinking about writing this chapter on viewpoint I remembered a book called *What About It Sharon?* by John Harvey, now sadly out of print. I was absolutely certain that this book would make an excellent example of the first person viewpoint. However, when I actually dug it out and re-read it, I realised that it isn't written in the first person at all, but third person singular:

> Debbie Bradley was a right bitch. A right little bitch! Walking round town with him like that. Strutting across from the fountain to the bus station on those stupid high heels of hers. It's a pity she didn't fall flat on her face, like the time she did when they went up to London on that visit.

The only clue we have that it isn't written in the first person is 'when *they* went up to London', which tells us we are not reading about personal experience.

Very generally speaking (there are no hard-and-fast rules when it comes to creative writing) I would suggest using third person singular for the more action-based story for the younger reader, and first person, perhaps, for the more introspective, character-led novel for the older reader. What I would *not* suggest doing is switching backwards and forwards between a number of different viewpoints simultaneously. Take the following snatch of dialogue:

'Have a good day at school, did we?' said Mrs Moore, thinking, not for the first time, how pretty her daughter would look if only she would smile more often.

'Not particularly,' said Debbie, slamming the front door behind her. She wondered why her mother couldn't make a perfectly simple enquiry without sounding sarcastic.

Mrs Moore sighed and turned back to the kitchen, leaving Debbie to sort herself out. She knew she'd only get even more angry otherwise. Debbie would leave her things strewn all over the hall, and guess who'd have to tidy it up later on?

Debbie fought back tears of frustration as she watched her mother's departing back. Her mother just wasn't interested in her.

'Tea's ready in half an hour,' said Mrs Moore.

That'd take the wind out of her sails. Usually she made Debbie get her own tea, but that extra half hour would give her time. She glanced towards the half empty bottle of gin on the kitchen side.

'Oh, see if I care!' she heard Debbie shout from the hall, followed by the familiar stamping of feet up the stairs.

This passage would work much better if written from one viewpoint only. As this is an excerpt from a children's story, the viewpoint character will have to be Debbie:

'Have a good day at school, did we?' said Debbie's Mum.

'Not particularly,' said Debbie, the welcoming smile she'd been going to give her mother freezing on her lips.

She slammed the door behind her and wondered, not for the first time, why her mother couldn't make a perfectly simple enquiry without sounding sarcastic.

'Mum . . .' she began, but her mother just sighed and went back into the kitchen.

Debbie hurled her things angrily across the hall floor, tears of disappointment and frustration stinging her eyes. Her mother just wasn't interested in her. All she cared about was herself. Herself and her precious drink.

She knew what her mother would be doing right now. She could see her stretching for the bottle of gin as if she were in the room with her.

'Tea's ready in half an hour,' said her Mum.

That surprised Debbie. Usually she had to get her own tea. She gave her school bag a kick and wondered, just for a moment, whether she should run into the kitchen. Say she was sorry. Talk to her about the drinking. But what was the point?

'See if I care!' she yelled, before stamping angrily up the stairs.

We learn the same information in this second passage but entirely from Debbie's point-of-view. Single-person viewpoint makes the passage more powerful and emotionally involving: less confusing. There is no mistaking which character the reader is supposed to identify with.

Multiple viewpoint is best reserved for straight adventure stories, where all the attention is focused on the action and we never really need to know what the characters are feeling and thinking. You can also use multiple viewpoint as a deliberate ploy, but you do need to structure your story in such a way that it doesn't become confusing. For example, if I had wanted to write from both Debbie's point-of-view and Mum's point-of-view I should have dealt with the two characters individually, making a distinct break whenever I changed viewpoint.

In *Flour Babies* Anne Fine begins the book from the teacher, Mr Cartright's, viewpoint. She then makes a break at the end of Chapter 1 and switches to the viewpoint of the main character, Simon Martin. If it is absolutely necessary to have more than one viewpoint, this is a much better way of handling the change.

In *Stone Cold* Robert Swindells uses first person multiple viewpoint; the book is written from the viewpoint of two different people, a homeless teenager and a serial killer. He alternates between the two and the switch is underlined by using two different typefaces for the two different characters. However, I should stress that it does take a great deal of skill to pull off a book written in this way. After all, you have two characters to know inside-out rather than one! For the inexperienced children's writer, it is simpler, wherever possible, to stick to the third person singular viewpoint.

Viewpoint: Exercise

- Write a conversation between two people, writing it first from both viewpoints; then from one viewpoint using third person singular; then from one viewpoint using first person. Which one comes most naturally to you? Which works the best?

CHAPTER FOURTEEN

STYLE

Beatrix Potter, Rudyard Kipling, A. A. Milne, Lewis Carroll – all the great children's writers have their own individual, very recognisable, style.

Who could mistake . . .

Once upon a time there were four little Rabbits, and their names were – Flopsy, Mopsy, Cotton-tail and Peter. They lived with their Mother in a sand-bank, underneath the root of a very big fir-tree.

. . . as anything other than Beatrix Potter?

Or . . .

Here is Edward Bear, coming downstairs now, bump, bump, bump on the back of his head, behind Christopher Robin.

. . . as anything other than A. A. Milne?

Many modern authors, too, have become known for their unique style – authors such as Roald Dahl, Philip Ridley, Paul Jennings, Dick King-Smith.

The temptation, for the new children's writer, is to copy the style of such authors rather than develop a style of their own. Sometimes this is done deliberately – particularly when the established author is dead: a new author admires an established author's books and decides to be the 'next' whoever it is.

But sometimes it is done subconsciously. After all, it makes sense that you are only going to want to write in a style which you, yourself, enjoy reading.

Either way, imitation of another author's writing style rarely works. You will be rumbled. Occasionally it may be possible to use elements of a recognisable style to help you develop a style of your own but, for the most part, style is something which it is almost impossible to imitate successfully.

Establishing a strong style is all-important. Very often an editor will admit that there is nothing particularly *wrong* with a submitted story but, when pushed to give a reason for rejecting it, will say, rather vaguely, 'It just wasn't *strong* enough' or 'It just wasn't *special* enough'. What they actually mean by this is that the writing didn't have a sufficiently individual style to make it stand out from all the other, equally satisfactorily mediocre, stories in the slush pile.

So how do you establish a unique style which is going to make an editor sit up and take notice?

BALANCE

The first thing which will discourage an editor – because it will consequently discourage a child – is pages and pages of uninterrupted narrative. Great blocks of text are boring to look at and a struggle to read.

So keep your paragraphs short, whatever age you are writing for, and make sure that you have a good balance of dialogue and narrative. Remember that dialogue when it goes on for too long can also become very confusing, as the reader tries to remember who is speaking. If you concentrate on establishing this ideal balance you will be forced to use dialogue only to move the plot forwards (or, occasionally, to reveal character).

The following was an opening to a short story sent to my editorial advice service by a new writer:

I was suddenly wide awake, but I could not work out why. I knew that, in my sleep, I had heard something but I didn't know what. I lay very still. There was nothing, not a sound. I waited a minute or two and then relaxed enough to turn over. At that moment it happened again, not loud, just a sort of drumming noise. It seemed to be coming from above my room, but there was nothing up there except the loft.

This is a very long, laboured first paragraph. The story went on:

It was the first night ever that I had been left alone in the house. Although I was thirteen several months ago, my parents did not want to leave me. Usually if they go out in the evening, my sister Sophie is here too. She's only ten and so I don't mind them fixing a baby-sitter. This time she had gone away with them to see our Gran who was ill, and I was allowed to stay here because of the big game the next day.

Dear me! I've almost forgotten why I'm reading this story. And still no sign of any dialogue . . .

I waited; it happened again. The only things in the loft are a few old cases and cardboard boxes of Christmas decorations, things like that. And, of course, the railway. My grandfather is mad about model trains. When Granny died – that's the other one, not the one who is ill at the moment – he moved into a special flat and so his railway moved here. I really enjoy running the trains too. But they don't run on their own in the middle of the night . . .

In fact, this is a potentially exciting and very tense situation, but any drama that might be there is completely submerged by the lengthy narrative. No editor would read beyond the first couple of pages. However, the author was determined that his story be accepted for publication and so we agreed to help him knock it into shape.

The first person viewpoint had to be dropped. This is an action-led story for eight-to twelve-year-olds and third person singular viewpoint is far more suitable for this type of story.

We suggested using shorter snappier sentences to grab the

attention and add punch, but also to increase the feeling of tension. As it stands, no emotion is being portrayed at all. Surely the boy would have been frightened?

A younger, more colloquial 'voice' was needed to tell the story. The opening above is grammatically correct, but it doesn't read like the voice of a fourteen-year-old boy.

The narrative needed to be broken up with dialogue, to move the story and add pace and momentum.

The author took our suggestions to heart, and a few days later we received version number two:

Nick sat bolt upright in bed. He'd heard a noise. He was sure of it. He reached under the bed for his baseball bat, then crept across his room to the open door.

'Who's that?' he shouted.

His voice echoed round the dark, empty house. But then he heard it again. That was it, a sort of rumbling, drumming noise. Where was it coming from, inside or outside? There it was again, up above, in the attic.

Nick took a deep, shaky breath. It was the first night that he'd been left alone in the house. Mum and Dad had gone to see Gran because she'd just been rushed into hospital and, of course, Sophie had gone too. There'd been quite a row because Mum had said he couldn't stay on his own, but it was the big game tomorrow, and he was captain.

'I'm fourteen, for heaven's sake,' he'd argued.

'Yes, let him stay,' Dad had agreed. 'There's got to be a first time. I'll make sure Bob's home this weekend.'

'Well, I'm still not happy,' said Mum, 'but if you promise to ring Uncle Bob if there's any problem, I suppose . . .'

Now Nick stood shaking in his bedroom doorway. He heard the noise again, right above his head.

'There's nothing in the attic except a few old cases and cardboard boxes, Christmas decorations, things like that,' he thought. 'And Grandpa's railway.'

The story, *Ghost Train* by John West, was accepted for publication by Orion Children's Books and included in an anthology of short stories in their Quids for Kids series. And you can see why.

SHOW DON'T TELL

In the first version of that story, there was too much long-winded 'telling' and not enough 'showing'.

'I was suddenly wide awake.' How can we visualise that? What happens when a person wakes from a deep sleep? Some people emerge slowly, floating between consciousness and unconsciousness for several minutes; others open their eyes suddenly and freeze. Others sit bolt upright, or leap out of bed. Whatever it is you think your character would do in this situation, it is far better, stylistically, to *describe* it to the reader, so they can get a detailed picture in their mind's eye of what happens. If someone is angry, *show* that they are angry. Perhaps their jaw is visibly clenched, or their fists. Perhaps their face has gone red, or white.

If someone is frightened, *show* it. We can clearly see, in the second version of the story, that Nick is frightened. He grabs his baseball bat. He takes a shaky breath. He stands shaking in his bedroom doorway. It is these little details which will add colour and depth to your writing and give your stories life.

A STYLE THAT FITS

Your writing style should suit the type of story that you're writing. If you are writing a contemporary 'real-life' story, then your writing style must have more punch and pace than if you are writing a historical drama, in which you need to capture the spirit of a bygone age.

Jill Paton Walsh uses a particularly distinctive writing style in *A Parcel of Patterns*, which tells the story of the plague, brought to the village of Eyam in a parcel of patterns from London:

> So I took my leave of her, and went home quiet and full of thought, and set about putting a rabbit to cook upon the spit, and to chopping the last few boughs of sage. Someone might yet have need of it. And now that Goody Trickett was lost, people came hoping to me, that I might know a little of what she knew. All my wisdom was sage tea; of that I made pansful.

Even if characters *didn't* speak like that back then – and we have no means of knowing – the idiom gives a distinct impression of another very different, time.

DON'T BE AFRAID OF SAID

I am always amazed at the endless alternatives new writers come up with to replace the word 'said'.

'Why not use "said?" she argued/gasped/demanded/muttered/ cried . . .

Sometimes I think writers are trying to prove that they have such a large vocabulary that they never need to use any verb more than once.

The fact is that the reader doesn't notice how many times an author uses 'he said/she said'. But the reader *will* notice – and remark upon its strangeness and artificiality – every time an alternative is used. 'Said' is hardly registered, except to tell the reader who is doing the speaking. That is the only reason it is there, after all. It is *what* is being said that the reader should be encouraged to focus on.

TITLES AND FIRST LINES

Titles and opening lines are more important than many of us like to believe. I'm not suggesting, for one minute, that it's something you should spend hours fretting over before you've written a single word. Indeed, the opposite may be true: finish your book first and *then* return to the opening pages. Often a title will only occur to you when you have written the book. When the book is finished, and your perspective is more objective, it is quite common to feel that the story would work better starting in a different place, or in a different way.

A writer once came to me at my Advice Centre, asking me to look at a book she had written for eight- to twelve-year-olds. Simultaneously she had also submitted the manuscript to a large publishing house where I happened to be doing some freelance work.

'What's Ruth's manuscript like?' I asked the editor she'd sent it to – I hadn't yet had a chance to look at it myself.

'I've had a quick glance at it,' the editor replied. 'Doesn't grab me.'

A few days later I cleared a space on my desk and started to read Ruth's manuscript. Because of what the editor said I wasn't hopeful.

As I began to read my worst fears were confirmed. The title of the story was *Summertime Santas*, which conjured up a Christmas story with a bit of summer-holiday adventure thrown in. Every editor's nightmare – a book with a seasonal theme and, therefore, a very limited sale. And the first chapter was toe-curdlingly amateurish.

However, I was being paid to assess this story and give editorial advice and assess it I would. Which meant reading the whole thing, no matter how awful it was.

But by the end of Chapter 2 I was hooked. I read the rest at one sitting. The first thing I did was pick up the phone and tell Ruth how wonderful I thought her story was and that I would do anything to see it published. But she'd have to lose the first chapter – and the title.

Eighteen months later that book was published by Puffin – the same publisher who had, originally, been doubtful. *The Master of Secrets* by Ruth Symes has been a great success.

The reason I am telling you this story is obvious. If I hadn't been paid to read the whole of that book I, as an editor, would never have got past the title and the first chapter. It would have joined the pile of rejections and the author would probably never have known the reason why.

I suppose you could say that this story is a lesson for publishers rather than authors. Ideally we should never give up on a book until we've read the whole thing. But this isn't an ideal world. Sadly editors don't have the time or resources to read more than the beginning – if that doesn't grab them, they'll abandon it. So try and ensure that your beginning 'hooks' the reader from the very first sentence. Establish tension, intrigue – make them want to read on, to find out what is going to happen. The title is equally important in the long run, as it will be used to sell the book to the customer; however, publishers will be prepared to come up with a title for you if they think your work has potential. But why not prove your talent by creating your own?

THE LAST WORD

New authors often worry about language. How complicated should the language they use be?

Stop worrying. This is only an issue when writing for the educational market. The language you use should be as simple as possible. You shouldn't simplify things to such an extent that you are patronising the child reader; but, on the other hand, you should be aware of words and sentence structures that children may not understand.

One of my students wrote a picture book based on the expression 'I've got the hump'. She insisted that it was an expression young children would understand. I had my doubts and asked my own children if they understood the expression. They didn't, but, I reasoned, they could be the exception rather than the rule. It wasn't until I was discussing the subject with another editor that the real problem became clear to me.

'It doesn't really matter whether some children understand the expression or not,' she pointed out. 'If there is *any doubt at all*, then don't use it.'

When writing for children you are aiming at clarity of expression. You are not trying to impress them with your intellectual achievements. If you write with the mind of a child (and the skill of an adult), you can't go far wrong.

Style: Exercises

- Think of some titles for any story ideas you may have. Would they make you want to read the book they are selling?
- Choose one of your ideas and write an eye-catching opening paragraph, making sure that it is your own unique voice you are using.

III

BEING
PUBLISHED

CHAPTER FIFTEEN

PRESENTATION AND APPROACH

The number of unsolicited manuscripts a publisher receives will depend on its profile and size. The smaller, lesser-known publishers receive maybe a few submissions a day, whereas large publishers may well receive hundreds a week. The one thing that *is* certain is that *all* publishers receive more unsolicited manuscripts than they would ideally like and some have a rather dismissive attitude to any unagented work.

But it needn't be this way. The only reason editors groan when faced with the slush pile is that so few unsolicited submissions reach even a minimum standard. Few writers research the market before approaching publishers (you already have a head start because you have read this book) – and that's not the worst omission by any means.

Sometimes the covering letter is so badly written that the editor knows the writer has no hope of being able to a construct a full-length story. Sometimes the manuscript is illegible – either because of bad handwriting or worn-out typewriter ribbon. Sometimes it's impossible to even open the envelope!

The main thing to remember when submitting a manuscript is not to give the publisher any excuse to reject your work without proper consideration. Publishers *want* to find good new writers, and readers and editors live in terror of missing the next blockbuster. All publishers have tales of rejecting books which went on to be bestsellers with another publishing house. If your work looks professional, your covering letter is intriguing and your submission fits the list of the publisher to whom you have sent it, you can be almost certain that it will not be cast aside completely unread. Presentation and approach are what it is all about.

RESEARCH THE MARKET

Researching the market you are writing for isn't just a case of relying on the few books that you have at home for your own children/grandchildren/pupils. Research requires some effort and I would expect a writer to have spent weeks, if not months, doing this research before even so much as *touching* a keyboard.

Buy, or borrow, as many titles as you can. Read them. Analyse them. Read them again . . . and again . . . and again! There is no substitute for reading as much current children's fiction as possible.

If you have been following this book section by section you will already have a good idea as to how to go about doing a certain amount of research through children's libraries and bookshops (and by completing the exercises listed at the end of each chapter). There is also a wide range of organisations and publications available designed to help people who want to become involved in the children's book world – more about these in the last chapter of this book.

Something else that you should be doing is collecting children's publisher's catalogues and editorial guidelines (if available). This is by far the best way of keeping in touch with the types of books that the different publishers are producing and will give you a good feel for the market. Catalogues are available, by request, from publisher's marketing departments and editorial guidelines from the relevant editorial department. A simple phone call should be enough to elicit these precious publications, although sometimes publishers prefer the request to be made in writing.

Once you have the information in front of you you need to analyse it carefully. Note the different profiles that publishers have. Some, such as Scholastic Children's Books, specialise in mass-market paperback fiction; others, like Oxford University Press, are essentially hardback publishers of more 'literary' children's fiction.

Note that I differentiate between paperback and hardback publishers. There was a time, in my early days of reading for Penguin Children's Books, when I would get quite cross if an author suggested submitting a manuscript to Puffin Books. 'Puffin is a *paperback* imprint,' I would irritably insist. 'New authors are always published by one of the hardback imprints first – if the title is successful, then, and *only* then, will it be taken on by Puffin.'

However, the times they are a-changin'. Penguin Children's Books have taken the decision to put the majority of their books straight into paperback and many other traditionally hardback publishers are going the same way.

You no longer need to worry so much, therefore, about which imprint to approach in any one publishing house (imprint is just another word for the separate divisions in publishing houses. For example at Penguin Children's Books has the Viking, Hamish Hamilton and Puffin imprints). If a publisher has hardback *and* paperback imprints it is probably still best to approach the hardback divisions first as they will take the decision on whether your work is best suited to hardback or paperback and pass it on to the relevant division. If they are solely a hardback publisher they will want to secure the paperback rights (so they can, hopefully, sell them onto another publishing house). If they are solely a paperback house then there are no problems.

PHONE CALLS, ENQUIRY LETTERS AND APPOINTMENTS

A common concern of any new writers is whether or not they should phone, or write to, a publisher *before* they submit any work. My general advice would be, don't. *All* publishers are keen to find good new writers – it is, after all, where their future profits lie. Even publishers who claim they do not consider unsolicited material, or who state that their lists are full, will make room for a new piece of work if they think it has commercial potential.

If you *do* make a phone call, remember that publishers'

offices are busy places and staff do not want to chat at length with total strangers. Get to the point quickly. Do not complain that the reader/editor is hard to get hold of (even if they are) and do not start by telling them how wonderful your story is (even if it is).

Take the opportunity to check the name of the editor to whom you should make the submission (and check the spelling of the name and address). If asked how long your story is do not say 'quite long', or 'quite short', or 'oh, about 72 pages'. After all it could be handwritten, typed, single-spaced, double-spaced, have two words per page, etc. Give the number of words – and count them *before* you make the call.

If asked what your story is about do not say: 'I would rather not give too much away/It is in the hands of my solicitor/The idea is patented'. Just give them an idea of the theme and style – as briefly as possible.

Enquiry letters are a complete waste of time unless you are requesting a catalogue or editorial guidelines. Letters that state, 'I have written a children's story. Would you be interested in look-ing at it?' are particularly pointless and will probably end up in the bin. After all, you should have enough confidence in your own work – and have researched the market sufficiently – to *know* that the publisher will be interested in looking at it.

No reader or editor will give you an appointment to see them unless they have first seen your work – they don't have the time. And don't turn up unannounced at their office and expect any-thing other than polite excuses – you will not get past the front desk.

If you are going to try an individual style of approach, do be careful. Sometimes these are intriguing; sometimes they are amateur at best.

For example, I once received a series of 'teasers', each one addressed specifically to me. They were colourful, professional computer print-outs, showing a football pitch with strap lines 'in the football vernacular' in large print:

I was sick as a parrot – unnamed source who missed out on Gillbert.
    The boy done good – the man who signed Gillbert.

Some of the crowd are on the pitch – advance order mayhem for Gillbert,
Gillbert ready for kick-off.

And, finally,

'Ere we go, 'ere we go, 'ere we go – Gillbert arrives on Monday.

And arrive it did, to earn my immediate attention. Sadly it wasn't quite right and was returned with a personal rejection letter:

Gillbert put on transfer market. Failed to live up to early potential – unnamed talent-spotter who picked up on Gillbert.

Another author tried similar but less appealing tactics which, as far as I was concerned, badly backfired.

I received, first, a rather poorly-made badge stating: *One Sandwich Short of a Picnic*; and secondly an empty sandwich packet in a jiffy bag. I found this approach at best, tasteless and, at worst, threatening. When I eventually received the manuscript I'm afraid I sent it straight back. I subsequently received a very unpleasant letter from the author complaining that I hadn't commented on his original approach.

If you don't feel you can pull off a 'PR stunt' successfully, then stick to more conventional tactics!

THE COVERING LETTER

'I have wrote this book . . .'

Atrocious English. But you would be amazed how many letters publishers receive from aspiring children's authors that start in exactly this way. Would it make you believe the author can write?

So the first thing to get right when approaching publishers with your work is the covering letter.

You *must* send one – it should be individually adapted to the requirements of each publisher you approach. It should be short (one A4 page), to the point and, preferably, typed. Remember to send it to a name (not Sir/Madam), to date it and sign it.

Bear in mind that publishers do *not* want to know who else has read your manuscript and enjoyed it – your granny, your neighbour's little girl, etc., and it is not a good idea to send copies of rejection letters from other publishers. Why let them know that other people don't want your work – unless it has had a very near miss and was ultimately rejected for reasons which won't make it less appealing elsewhere.

The other thing that publishers don't want to read in a covering letter is your life history. Some writers seems to find it necessary to impart the minutest details about whey they wrote the book in the first place, their personal circumstances, their state of health ... On the other hand there is a happy medium to be struck – one letter I received the other day simply said, 'A 10,000-word Christmas story. Any chance?'

Other 'don't's' in the covering letter: *don't* say that you have written 'a series of children's books' (unless it's been published!) or state that your idea has enormous potential for merchandising – and that you have already designed the T-shirt and stuffed the cuddly toy. No publisher will take on a series until the first book has been a proven success. And to come up with an idea for merchandising before acceptance is jumping the gun by a very long way.

A covering letter should say what your story is about (one line), how long it is (number of words) and how you think it will fit into the publisher's programme. It should also mention in passing any previously published work or other relevant experience.

Here is an example of a covering letter which, if all else fails, I suggest you use as a template:

```
(Date)

(Address)

Dear Editor (use full name)

I enclose my manuscript The Wizard's Skip.

This is a humorous, fantasy adventure
story for five to eight year-olds and is
```

about a boy who finds a video game in a
skip. It is 3000 words in length and I
see it fitting into your Banana Book
series.

I am a teacher by training and have
three children of my own, all under ten.
I have had a few articles published in
local publications and edit our church
newsletter. This is my first children's
book.

I look forward to hearing your reactions to *The Wizard's Skip*.

Yours sincerely,

(Name)

MANUSCRIPT PRESENTATION

Your manuscript should be typed (preferably double-spaced), as
error-free and clean as possible, using one side of A4 white paper
only. It doesn't have to be prepared on a state-of-the-art computer but, if you are going to write seriously, you will probably
want to invest in some kind of word processor. Second-hand
machines can be bought inexpensively these days and once you
have one you will wonder how you ever managed without.

Your manuscript should not be bound, stapled or paper-
clipped – particularly annoying is when authors paper-clip or
staple each individual chapter, making them unmanageable to
read. I suggest putting the manuscript loose in a strong cardboard
or plastic folder. Label the front of the folder with the title of the
manuscript and your name and address. Put your name and
address on the title page, together with the number of words.
Number the pages and put your name and address on the last
page of the manuscript.

If you are submitting a longer novel – anything over 15,000
words – I suggest enclosing the first three or four chapters and a
brief synopsis. By a synopsis I do mean just that – not a chapter-
by-chapter outline. All editors really want to know, if they like

the first few chapters, is the direction the story is going to take. If they want to know what happens chapter by chapter they will ask for the rest of the manuscript.

If your story is under 15,000 words I would suggest sending the whole thing, perhaps with a synopsis for good measure.

If it is a picture book it is a good idea to enclose a dummy, a separate copy of the text divided into pages and a copy of the text 'straight' (ie. undivided).

Don't worry about copyrighting your work. Some authors go to the most extraordinary lengths to protect their submissions but, contrary to popular belief, publishers are not in the habit of stealing ideas. It isn't possible to copyright an idea anyway and, if anyone is going to steal anything, it will be the concept rather than the written text.

REJECTION

Be prepared for it!

Enclose return postage. Publishers simply cannot be expected to fund return postage of manuscripts for the hundreds of unsolicited submissions they receive.

Either enclose an envelope or packaging ready stamped and addressed, or send stamps together with, preferably, a sticky self-addressed label. Personally I prefer the latter – it removes the temptation for an editor to pop your manuscript straight into the return envelope without even looking at it!

It is reasonable to expect a publisher to take anything up to three months to consider your work so it is perfectly acceptable to approach more than one publisher at once with the same piece of work. However, you should tell each publisher that you have done this. This is because publishers often sit on author's manuscripts for longer than they should, and knowing that someone else is also looking at the work tends to awaken the publisher's competitive instincts and speed a decision.

Authors tend to worry that, if they do approach more than one publisher at once, they will receive multiple offers and upset people all round. All I can say to that is, you should be so lucky!

Rejection letters are usually fairly standard. A publisher seldom has the time to give you a specific reason for rejection so letters will often include polite and largely meaningless phrases such as 'we enjoyed your work but I'm afraid it isn't quite right for us'. If you do get a personally-worded rejection letter (and do remember that a letter can often *look* personal but be 'mass-produced') take it in the spirit in which it is intended. It is all too easy to react with anger to criticism, but an editor wouldn't take the trouble to give that criticism if they didn't feel that your writing showed promise. If you really can't stomach the advice then put the letter away for a few days/weeks/months until you feel you can go and look at it with some objectivity. *Don't*, whatever you do, let the editor know that you are angry. You would be amazed at how many abusive letters editors receive from rejected authors. Making an enemy of an editor can only harm you in the long run, and, in any case, it is unreasonable to be unpleasant to someone simply for doing their job.

Often criticism will be backed up with a phrase such as 'we would be happy to see more of your work'. Again, take this in the spirit in which it is meant. Don't just post off another story which you happen to have on file but work on something new, specifically targeted at that publisher, and send it in as soon as you can. When you do so, remind the editor of who you are and what it was you sent in last time. They won't necessarily remember, but they will know that if they said they wanted to see more of your work they liked your original submission.

There are many reasons for rejection. It could be because your writing isn't good enough – but it could be because the publishers already have a similar story on their list. Alternatively it could be down to personal taste. All editors try to be objective, but they are bound to look more favourably on material that they themselves enjoy.

Sometimes an editor will tell you that your work wasn't 'strong' enough. An agent friend of mine believes that, when an editor says that, it's a sure sign that they haven't read the manuscript. I disagree. When most editors say something isn't strong enough they mean just that there's nothing wrong with it, but it has nothing sufficiently special to make it stand out from the competition.

Try to turn rejection into a positive learning experience. One writer I know received a simply-worded rejection letter from an editor saying that she liked the story but 'it wasn't quite right.' She would have thought no more of it had the editor not mistakenly also enclosed her report on the story for the editorial meeting. It was extremely damning!

However, once she'd recovered from the shock (and it took her several days, if not weeks), she read and re-read that report, taking every single comment on board. Her feeling was that this unfortunate oversight had occurred for a reason – and that reason was to make her a better writer.

She has now published six books, with six more in the pipeline.

CHAPTER SIXTEEN

ACCEPTANCE

Acceptance of your book for publication is every author's dream. It is what you have been striving for. It is the reason you wrote it. It is the reason you have worked so hard completing all the exercises in this book! It doesn't matter how much you tell yourself that you enjoy writing for its own sake – the fact is we all want formal recognition for what we do, and an offer of publication provides that recognition.

Every writer who has submitted a manuscript to a publisher waits with baited breath for some kind of response. The post is eyed warily every day. Is that big, bulky package your returned manuscript? If no bulky package arrives, then does that nice, clean, white envelope contain the offer of your dreams?

Forget it. It's more than likely that the process of acceptance will take a much more complicated and lengthy route.

Often it will be a question of building up a relationship with an editor over a long period of time. It may start with a personal rejection letter saying that, although this particular manuscript isn't quite right, they would be happy to see more of your work. More work duly wings its way in the right direction and, after perhaps another rejection or two, the editor may invite you in for 'a chat'.

All publishers (and agents) need to assess the marketability of their authors. They need to know that you don't have only one book in you, that if they publish your book you will be able to provide more work of the same standard. They want to be reassured that you are committed as a writer, that you are versatile and that, as a personality, you are someone they can work with. They want to know whether – and how – they can promote you as an author. They are, in short, looking on you as an investment – because that's exactly what you are. Few first books make money, so the publisher needs to be sure that, even if they lose money on your first book, they are going to have more than one bite at the apple.

For this reason publishers don't like their authors spreading themselves too thinly. They like authors to be loyal to them, and them alone. So if you get as far as the 'chatting' stage – even if you know that you are planning to work with other publishing houses – be as positive and as upbeat as possible. It's a bit like a job interview – ultimately you don't *have* to take the job, but you need to give the impression that you want it more than any other.

Even after the interview is over you will probably still not have a promise of a formal offer. The editor may ask you to do some more work on your manuscript – or may suggest that you try writing a completely different book for a specific slot. If I were you I would go along with the editor for as long as you feel is reasonable. After all, as an unpublished writer, you have nothing to lose.

The only time to start talking money is if they ask to take your book to one of the book fairs. At that stage it may be reasonable to ask for some kind of development fee and, to be fair, most reputable publishers will offer this without you having to ask.

However, as far as revising manuscripts is concerned, I'm afraid that is just part and parcel of being a new writer. A publisher is under no obligation to accept your work, even after *hundreds* of rewrites, if they still don't like it. Most publishers, in any case, don't have the time to encourage authors unless they genuinely feel that both sides are going to benefit at the end of it all.

OFFER

The day comes. The offer letter finally arrives. All your hard work has been worthwhile and you are about to become a published children's author at last.

Wrong!

I don't want to be negative, but I have seen too many

disappointed authors not to offer a few words of warning at this stage. *Nothing* is certain in publishing until you have the published book in your hands. I have seen contracts signed, advances paid – and *still* the book has been cancelled.

I had a phone call from one author the other day who had been excitedly waiting for the publication day of her first picture book. She'd been paid the advance, she'd approved the cover and the illustrations, she'd seen her name appear in the catalogue – she'd done everything, except see the finished copy. And then, four weeks before publication date, the foreign publisher with whom a co-edition had been lined up cancelled the contract, and the whole deal collapsed. To say she was disappointed would be an understatement!

It probably won't happen to you, but it *might*. Forewarned is forearmed.

The offer letter will generally get straight to the point. It will say that the publisher likes your book and is happy to make an offer to publish it. It will offer an advance, set against royalties, usually payable in two (or sometimes three) stages – half on signature of the contract and half on publication, or one third on signature, one third on acceptance of the typescript in a state ready for publication, and one third on actual publication. An advance is literally that – the publisher is advancing you potential earnings. You will not receive royalties (ie. a percentage of the sale price of each book sold) until the advance has 'earned out' – in other words, until your book has earned more money for the publisher than your advance was worth.

The letter will also talk about rights. Usually nowadays the offer is likely to cover both hardback and paperback rights, but the publisher will also want to 'control' other rights, meaning that they can sell the book to other markets – in America, in translation, to large print publishers, to magazines . . . Agents tend to hang on to these rights on behalf of their authors and then do the selling themselves but if you don't have an agent a publisher will expect what is called 'world rights'. You will be given a percentage of every additional rights sale made by your publisher or agent.

The letter will probably mention a provisional timescale – when they would like delivery of the completed text, and when they plan to publish the book.

The next move is down to you. You can either accept straight away (and if it's your first book you'll be very tempted!), or you can give the offer a little thought (and then accept it), or you can negotiate on any points that concern you. But remember that despite every inexperienced author's belief that all publishers are out to 'do' the writer, most publishers have very standard terms and conditions for books that they take on to their list.

The first thing you will realise is that you won't get rich quick by writing for children. On average an advance for a first book will be between £500 and £2000, depending on the type and length of the book. This is set against royalties which are, again, fairly standard – say between 7 and 8 per cent of the published price on hardback sales and less on paperback sales (because more will be sold). A royalty isn't always on offer. For short stories a flat fee is usually paid (which can often seem derisory) and the author will rarely see any additional income.

You are perfectly entitled to try to 'up' the advance if you feel it is too low. However, as most publishers offer standard amounts and don't expect to make much of a profit on a new writer in any case, there is usually little room for negotiation. The bottom line, with a first book, is that the publisher holds all the cards. And they can always cancel if they feel you are being difficult. If you have good reason to believe that the terms you are being offered are genuinely unreasonable then do take it up with them – as politely as possible! The Society of Authors will advise you on this – more about them later.

The one area of the offer letter which you can negotiate on is the timescale factor. More often than not with a first book, you will already have written the complete text and it will be a case of revision only. However, even revision can take time, so do make sure that you can deliver on the date that they say. It is much better to ask for more time at this early stage than to let publishers down at the last minute, when your book has already been scheduled.

THE CONTRACT

Once you have negotiated the basic terms you will, at some stage, be sent a formal contract to sign, after which you usually receive half of the advance payable. I say 'at some stage' because it can seem like forever before the contract actually arrives, and even longer before you receive any money. Often you will be well along the road to publication before you see any sign of a contract.

The whole subject of contracts is too vast and complicated to be covered in a book like this, so I will just mention a few points to look out for:

Do read your contract from start to finish, even if you think it looks too complicated for you to understand. Even though, as mentioned above, most publishers have standard contracts, don't feel that you can't query clauses, or make changes to the contract (within reason).

Obviously you need to check that the delivery date is the same as the one you discussed after receiving your offer letter, and think again whether it is reasonable for you.

If your work has been commissioned but not yet accepted in its completed form be very careful over any wording alluding to the publisher having no obligation to accept the finished work if deemed unacceptable. It is right and proper that a publisher should have an escape clause if they have misjudged the capabilities of the author – but to be fair to the author they must be able to justify their rejection and give the author the opportunity to bring their work up to standard.

Don't agree to the publisher being able to edit your work without your approval. When Malorie Blackman's picture book *That New Dress* was published in the States, the American publisher wanted to change the last three words of the book from 'And Mum smiled' to 'And Mum sighed'. This was a tiny change but, in fact, changed the whole ending of the book from satisfactory to rather unsatisfactory. It's a point worth bearing in mind – remember just how crucial even small changes can be.

Watch out for any clauses giving the publisher the right to publish the author's next work. Contracts usually do contain this clause and, whilst publishers may not agree to remove it, at least get them to ensure that the clause doesn't act to the detriment of you, the author. One author I know agreed to just such a clause and then, after publication of his first book (which was very successful), found that the publisher wouldn't either agree or disagree to publish another book. They stalled on everything that he offered them but, because of the terms of his contract, he couldn't threaten to take his work elsewhere.

Rights is another section of the contract which authors get hot under the collar about, particularly in this electronic age when audio, radio, television, film, video, animation and electronic multimedia rights are all assuming greater importance than they used to. In fact, some contracts still don't make specific provision for some of these rights. Remember that the selling of various rights is just another way in which you and your publisher can make money from your book. If you don't have an agent to sell the rights for you, then the publisher will undertake to do it. They will want to sell the rights – and generate extra income – as much as you do! It is just worth checking whether they can sell rights without consulting you first to get your agreement on any rights deal.

If you are concerned about your contract, and don't have anyone to advise you, my suggestion would be that you join The Society of Authors (see page 167). You can become a provisional member for around £60 (for the first year) and their legal team will vet the contract for you. This means that you are getting legal advice for a reasonable fee from someone who knows a great deal about publishing contracts – which are quite different from any contract you've ever seen before. They also publish a very good *Quick Guide to Publishing Contracts* which is inexpensive and written by experts.

WORKING TOWARDS PUBLICATION

To start with you will be assigned an editor who will work with you on revisions and changes. It is important to build up a good relationship with your editor and to trust his or her judgement. If you don't agree with any changes, then say so, but try not to quibble unless you feel particularly strongly about a change. If your objections are reasonable it is more than likely that your editor will agree with you – or have a very good reason not to. However, there is absolutely no point in establishing a reputation for being what every editor dreads: a 'difficult author'. In that case your publisher will only be less likely to want to work with you again.

If your book is a picture book or heavily illustrated Reader, you may be consulted on the choice of illustrator. But as a general rule the publisher is the best judge of which illustrative style best suits your text. Even if you had your heart set on one particular illustrator, the chances are that they may not necessarily have the time to fit in with the publishing schedule. Often it is a question of trying two or three illustrators before one finally works out in every respect.

As far as the book jacket is concerned you will be shown it for approval, but as a formality more than anything else, unless the right to approve jacket artwork is written into your contract (and publishers rarely agree to this – they feel they are in a better position to know what sort of jacket will sell your book than you are, which is probably true). You should check, however, that all the details are correct – including the 'blurb' on the back of the book. It has been known for publishers to get names wrong and just occasionally the story is totally unrecognisable.

Another time when you need to be alert to the possibility of mistakes is when you receive the proofs. Proofs are unbound copies of the final book and because all the typesetting has been done and the illustrations are in place it is important not to make any drastic changes (indeed your contract will probably make you liable for the cost if you do). But if you spot any mistakes, then speak up.

PUBLICATION

One thing that many new authors forget is that publication of a book doesn't happen instantly. The gap between an offer being made and actual publication is often as much as eighteen months to two years. It always makes me laugh when, around November time, I start receiving stories with a view to publication that Christmas! It just isn't humanly possible, I'm afraid.

You will receive an advance copy 'hot off the press' prior to publication of your book and, once it is actually on the bookshop shelves, you should receive complimentary – or 'gratis' – copies for your own distribution to family and friends. Do remember to keep at least a couple of copies of your book for yourself. It is unlikely, as a first book, that it will have a long shelf life and it could well be out of print within a few years. Once that happens it will be impossible to get hold of more copies, and it's always good to be able to show future publishers samples of published work.

How well your book is marketed will depend on how good your publisher's marketing and sales teams are. The marketing team will promote your book in any way they think appropriate – firstly by ensuring that it is included in their catalogue. Children's publishing catalogues generally come out on an annual basis and include all the books that will be published by them during that year.

The marketing team will also try to persuade all the relevant critics to review your work although this isn't always easy with children's books, and even less easy for a new author.

The sales team will work on getting retail outlets to stock your books – although, again, this isn't always easy. Large book chains know that only the high-profile children's authors sell in any great quantities, so it may be a case of using persuasive powers or smaller bookshops and specialist children's bookshops.

There is a certain amount of promotion you can do yourself.

Contact local bookshops (who may be keen to stock your book if you are available for signing sessions and if your publisher can provide showcards), speak to local schools to arrange author visits, go to local libraries to arrange author visits, and send details of your book and yourself to local papers, radio stations and regional TV. The more you can promote yourself, the more copies of your book you are going to sell.

ROYALTIES

To start with you won't earn any royalties because you'll still be earning your advance. However, you will receive royalty state-ments (twice a year usually, or as specified in your contract) which will show how quickly your advance is being earned. Once it has earned out, and assuming that your book is still sell-ing, you will receive twice-yearly royalty cheques – but these may only be for a few pounds!

If you don't have an agent to check your royalty statements for you, check them carefully yourself. Again The Society of

Authors can help with this task. If, after two years or so, the sales are very low, or down to nil, a reprint may well be in order. If not, ask your editor why not? A decision to reprint has to be taken with some care as far as the publisher is concerned and if, after discussion, they decide not to reprint you can ask for the book rights to revert to you. Who knows – after several years, if the time is right, someone may be keen to bring out a new edition.

VANITY PUBLISHING

Authors come to me every week claiming to have had offers to publish their work. Often these 'offers' turn out to be from subsidy or 'vanity' publishers, rather than mainstream publishers.

What is the difference, you may well ask? Thousands of pounds, I would answer. Of your money.

They are open to all-comers and are non-selective. They will publish anything, so long as you are prepared to put up enough money. The best of them only require enough money to cover their costs and make a small profit; the worst are professional fraudsters and will demand huge sums, for which you will receive very little. These vanity publishers provide editorial reports on manuscripts submitted to them which are works of fiction in themselves. The reports are glowing and are designed to be a means of extracting your money. Don't be fooled. If your work is good enough to win commercial success it will be taken on by a mainstream publisher – and they will pay *you* for the privilege of being able to publish.

CHAPTER SEVENTEEN

HELP!

Writing is a very isolating experience. It doesn't matter how experienced you are – you will always feel, to a certain extent, alone. However, for children's writers, there is plenty of ongoing support available.

AGENTS

Many children's writers are desperate to enlist the help of an agent. This isn't, necessarily, because they feel that agents are the only route to success: more that they see agents as someone to relive the loneliness of being a writer. They imagine them as being a combination of editor, therapist and friend all rolled into one. And they also believe that an agent will help them negotiate their way through the minefield of contracts – and find them a publisher in the first place.

Agents are *not* the answer to the new author's prayers. For a start, few reputable agents are prepared to take a new author onto their list until that author has some published work under his or her belt. And it *isn't* a 'chicken and egg' situation. Almost *all* new writers break into children's publishing *without* the help of an agent. It is only agents themselves who would have you believe that this isn't the case!

Even if you do persuade an agent to take you on you will, until you have some experience and confidence in your own abilities, find that your agent is just another hoop to jump through. Under the terms of your agreement with your agent, you will almost certainly have to submit all work to publishers through him or her and, because as a new author you come low on their list of priorities, it can sometimes take an agent a long time to give you any sort of reaction to your work.

In the meantime your hands are tied. And if, eventually, they come back to you with a negative response and refuse to submit your work to a publisher, you are completely stuck. You *have* to trust their judgement if you want to stay with them – but, on the other hand, you will be itching to submit your work to publishers, no matter what your agent says.

Nevertheless, if you find an agent you respect, you can build a creative and beneficial relationship. A good agent will devote time and energy to making your book as good as it can be. Once it reaches the publisher it will unquestionably be looked at with more speed than if it had simply joined the slush pile of unsolicited work. A good agent will also keep you in touch with current publishing requirements which will, inevitably, put you ahead of the game. And the best agents will have the pulling power to be able to negotiate larger advances.

My advice would be not to waste time trying to find an agent until you have had your first acceptance. Then I would suggest approaching a couple of agents and seeing what reaction you get.

If an agent does express an interest in taking you onto their list, do make sure that you meet them first, to assess whether or not you feel you could work closely with them. Check out their credentials and approach. Ask whether they are prepared to share their experience and creativity with authors, providing full editorial guidance, or whether they simply send manuscripts out to publishers 'untouched'. Ask how long they take, on average, to respond to authors with criticism and advice. Ask if they will regularly 'touch base' with you to let you know of any developments, and to tell you what sort of books children's publishers are currently looking for. Ask if they will keep you informed about the submissions they make, and whether, once you have forged a relationship with a particular editor, they are happy for you to work with that person direct without using the agent as a 'go-between'. And – most importantly – ask what percentage they will demand should they sell your book! Ten percent of any sales made is acceptable – anything much above this, and you should think twice. Leave no stone unturned – after all, you will be entrusting your precious work to this person, and you must be able to think that they are doing their very best for you.

BOOKS

If you haven't done so already, there are several books I would suggest adding to your writer's library which will be of invaluable assistance to you:

The Writers' and Artists' Yearbook (A & C Black).
This is updated annually and has an excellent section on writing for children written by leading children's literary agent, Caroline Sheldon.

The Writers' Handbook (Macmillan)
Most writers have one or the other of the above. However, if money is no object, I would suggest keeping both for reference purposes. The layout of *The Writers Handbook* is slightly easier on the eye.

The Waterstone's Guide to Children's Books
This is an excellent catalogue of books being published for children. It is divided into age and subject categories and combines brief book reviews with interesting snippets of information about authors and is available from branches of Waterstones priced £1.99.

The Children's Book Handbook
This is an invaluable resource guide for everyone connected with children's writing. It contains details of organisations concerned with children's books, courses, prizes, awards, competitions, publishers, the most popular books of the previous year – and much more.

Available annually from *Young Book Trust, Book House, 45 East Hill, London SW18 2QZ.*

PUBLICATIONS

As well as books there are a number of magazines on sale which are very helpful to the children's writer:

Writing Magazine and Writers News
Writing Magazine is available bi-monthly on the newsstands; *Writers News*, from the same stable, is available by subscription only. Both contain interesting features on all aspects of writing, including articles specifically targeted at children's writers. They also contain information on writing circles and writing courses.

For subscription details contact: *Writers News Ltd, PO Box 4, Nairn IV12 4HU.*

Books for Keeps
This is an excellent magazine aimed at everyone interested in children's books. It comes out bi-monthly and is full of book reviews, articles, authorgraphs, etc. If you were going to subscribe to one magazine and no other this is the one I would choose.

By subscription from: *Books for Keeps, 6 Brightfield Road, Lee, London SE12 8QF.*

Carousel
This magazine is similar to *Books for Keeps* except it is available three times a year (ie once a term) only. It has strong connections with The Federation of Children's Book Groups (mentioned below).

By subscription from: *Carousel, 7 Carrs Lane, Birmingham B4 7TQ.*

Signal: Approaches to Children's Books
Again available three times a year and very much for the dedicated children's writer. It contains academic 'essays', as opposed to articles, on all topics related to children's publishing. A variety of people contribute to this publication, including authors and editors.

By subscription from: *Thimble Press, Lockwood, Station Road, South Woodchester, Stroud, Glos. GL5 5EQ.*

The Junior Bookshelf

This isn't a glossy, colourful publication but it is full of useful reviews of children's books. It is available six times a year.

By subscription from: *Marsh Hall, Thurstonland, Huddersfield, HD4 6XB.*

The Bookseller

This magazine, available weekly from newsagents, is gradually becoming more orientated towards the children's books world. As well as the occasional round-up of children's publishing in a section entitled 'Children's Book News', it is also now producing a *Children's Bookseller* twice a year. It is expensive to buy on a weekly basis but if you can find out when the *Children's Bookseller* will be appearing it might be worth ordering a copy of that particular edition.

For details contact: *The Children's Bookseller, 12 Dyott Street, London WC1A 1DF.*

ORGANISATIONS

A number of organisations have been mentioned in passing throughout this book: here's more information on those which are most useful for the new writer.

Young Book Trust

Part of Book Trust, this charitable trust offers a children's book information service. Their library, situated in Book House, holds every children's book published in the past two years. If you become a member of Young Book Trust, you will receive useful mailings throughout the year. This includes their news magazine and also a free copy of *The Children's Book Handbook* (mentioned above) and other useful publications.

Details from: *Young Book Trust, Book House, 45 East Hill, London SW18 2QZ.*

The Children's Book Circle

This organisation provides a discussion forum for anybody interested in children's books. Six meetings a year are addressed by a panel of speakers on a chosen topic and usually take place at children's publishing houses in Central London.

Membership enquiries to: *Gaby Morgan, Macmillan Children's Books, 25 Eccleston Place, London SW1W 9NF.*

The Federation of Children's Book Groups
Like the Children's Book Circle, this is an organisation for all those involved in children's books. However, it has a more national flavour and organises a large annual conference.

Membership enquiries to: *Children's Book Groups, 7 Carrs Lane, Birmingham, B4 7TQ.*

The Society of Authors
You will not be able to become a member of this society until you have had a formal publishing offer for a book. However, once this happens, it is a very useful organisation. As mentioned previously, it offers a free contract advisory service and also produces a journal, *The Author*, which is full of information, articles and publishing news.

Enquiries to: *The Society of Authors, 84 Drayton Gardens, London SW10 9SB.*

TRAINING AND ADVICE

You can, of course, join a local writer's circle. These circles tend to meet on a regular basis and members take it in turns to read out their work. Personally I wouldn't recommend this route unless the writing circle you choose specialises in children's writing. If other members know nothing about children's publishing you will almost certainly get an inaccurate view of your work which may harm, rather than help, any future success.

However, there are plenty of other places where you can go for training and advice.

The Arvon Foundation
This organisation offers writers the opportunity to live and work with professional authors. It runs a large variety of writing courses, including writing for children, at three centres in Devon, Yorkshire and Scotland. The accommodation tends to be on the basic – and over-crowded – side, but any discomfort is well worth enduring for the excellence of the course content.

Details from: *Arvon Foundation, Totleigh Barton, Sheepwash, Beaworthy, Devon EX21 5NS.*

The Newydd Writing Courses

I have no personal experience of this organisation but have heard very good reports from other writers. It runs courses on writing for children with support from the Welsh Arts Council.

Details from: *Taliesin Trust, Tyy Newydd, Llanystumdwy, Cricieth, Gwynedd LL52 0LW.*

The City Literary Institute

This is an adult education college and provides a wide variety of part-time writing courses for adult and children's writers.

Details from: *The City Literary Institute, 16 Stukeley Street, London WC2B 5LJ.*

The Writers Advice Centre for Children's Books

This organisation (run by me!) is the only one of its kind in the country. It is open to all-comers and offers individual editorial and marketing advice to children's writers on a fee-paying basis.

We have collected together a team of editorial readers, all of whom currently work in children's publishing, and we also run day courses throughout the year, and are planning a home study course in conjunction with *Writers News*.

To our more promising authors, who have used the advice service first, we do offer a limited agency service.

Further details from: *The Writers Advice Centre, Palace Wharf, Rainville Road, London W6 9HN. Tel 0181-874 7347.*

AND LASTLY ...

A speaker on one of our Writers Advice Centre courses recently brought me up short. He reminded us all that, no matter what books we read, no matter how many courses we go to, no matter how many publishers we speak to, the only people who really matter when we are writing for children are the children themselves.

So, as well as involving yourself in the children's book world, involve yourself with children. Expand your research to include books on child development and child psychology.

And always bear in mind that writing – any kind of writing – is a craft. Like all crafts, it takes time and hard work to perfect. I have seen many authors over the years and I have learnt, through experience, success isn't a question of talent – at least, not only talent. Above all, it's a question of perseverance.

A very famous artist, in his eighties and dying, was still working on a canvas. When asked what he was doing he replied, 'I'm learning'. That's how it should be for you. A writer, like an artist, never stops learning, no matter what stage he or she is at. I truly believe that those authors who want to make it will do so in the end. It's a question of learning from experience, believing in your own abilities, and never, ever, giving up.

Good luck!

PRIZES AND AWARDS

There are only two national awards for new, unpublished children's authors, and only one for unpublished illustrators. So let's start with those.

The Fidler Award
Previously called The Kathleen Fidler Award and sponsored by Blackie Books (now defunct), this award is currently sponsored by Hodder Children's Books.

It is an annual award designed to encourage good new fiction for the 8–12 age range from unpublished writers. To enter writers have to be unpublished and unagented and books have to be between 20–25,000 words.

There is a cash prize of £1000 and Hodder undertake to publish the winning entry.

Past winners have included *Run Zan Run* by Catherine MacPhail (1994), *Edge of Danger* by Clare Dudman (1995) and *Falcon's Quest* by John Smirthwaite (1996).

The award is administered by Book Trust Scotland. Further details, plus an application form, can be obtained by sending an sae to *Book Trust Scotland, Scottish Book Centre, 137 Dundee Street, Edinburgh E11 1BG.*

The Independent/Scholastic Story of the Year Competition
This competition is open to anyone, published or unpublished, and was set up to find original short stories for the 6–9 age

group. It is run by the *Independent* newspaper and Scholastic Children's Books, with the *Independent* running all the publicity and Scholastic publishing the winners and runners-up in an annual anthology, *Story of the Year.*

Full details can either be found in the *Independent* around March/April or, alternatively, by writing to *The Publicity Department, Scholastic Children's Books, Commonwealth House, 1–19 New Oxford Street, London WC1A 1NU.*

The Macmillan Prize

This is an award for work which the judges consider to show great potential within the field of children's book illustration. The award was established in 1984 to stimulate new work from illustrators in art schools. Pan Macmillan has the option to use the work of the prizewinners.

Further details can be obtained by writing to *Macmillan Children's Books, 25 Eccleston Place, London SW1W 9NF.*

As well as these large national competitions, it is always worth looking out for smaller local versions as these can help you establish a regional reputation – and if you win it won't do your 'CV' any harm!

A number of recognised awards have been set up in children's publishing. Until you are published, this list is going to hold more relevance for research purposes than anything else – all children's writers should be aware of, and have read, the major award winners of each year. If they've won an award, they must be getting something right!

Angus Book Award

This is an initiative to encourage pupils to read quality teenage fiction. From January to March third-year pupils read and assess the five shortlisted titles, chosen by teachers and librarians from books published in paperback in the preceding twelve months and written by an author resident in the UK. The books are discussed in class before the children vote in a secret ballot.

Past winners include *Night After Tomorrow* by Sue Welford.

The Caldecott Medal

This award, instituted in 1938, is presented for the most distinguished American picture book for children published during the preceding year.

Past winners have included *Officer Buckle and Gloria* by Peggy Rathman and *Smoky Night* by David Diaz Jovanovich and Eve Bunting.

The Carnegie Medal

The Carnegie Medal is given for an outstanding book for children. Contenders are appraised for characterisation, plot, style, accuracy, imaginative quality and that indefinable element that lifts the book above the competition.

Past winners have included *Stone Cold* by Robert Swindells, *Whispers in the Graveyard* by Theresa Breslin and *Northern Lights* by Philip Pullman.

The Kate Greenaway Medal

This goes to an artist who has produced distinguished work in the illustration of children's books. The nominated books are assessed for design, format and production as well as artistic merit.

Past winners have included *Way Home* by Gregory Rogers and *The Christmas Miracle of Jonathan Toomey* by P. J. Lynch.

The Children's Book Award

This award has been made annually since 1980 and is organised by The Federation of Children's Book Groups. It is judged by children themselves and thousands of children from all over the country help to test the books in order to find 'the best book of the year'. Information about the year's books collected during testing is compiled into a 'pick of the year' booklist of tried and tested books.

The lists are well worth collecting and are available, for a fee, from *The National Secretary – FCBG, 6 Bryce Place, Currie, Edinburgh EH14 5LR*.

Earthworm Children's Book Award
The Earthworm Award has been set up by Friends of the Earth to encourage writing of children's books which reflect concern about environmental issues.

Past winners include *Project Kite* by Sian Lewis.

Guardian Children's Fiction Award
This is for outstanding works of fiction for children and is chosen by a panel of authors and the *Guardian* children's books review editor. Picture books are not included.

Past winners have included *Maphead* by Lesley Howarth and *The Mennyms* by Sylvia Waugh.

Hans Christian Andersen Award
This is given by the International Board on Books for Young People (IBBY) to an author and illustrator whose works have made an important contribution to children's literature.

Past winning authors have been Virginia Hamilton, Michio Mado and Uri Orlev. Past winning illustrators have been Kveta Pacovska, Jorg Muller and Klaus Ensikat.

The Kurt Maschler Award
This award was established in 1982 by the late Kurt Maschler for a work of imagination in the children's field in which excellent text and illustration are presented so that each enhances, yet balances, the other.

Past winners have been *Drop Dead* by Babette Cole and *The Little Boat* by Kathy Henderson and Patrick Benson.

Lancashire County Library Children's Books of the Year Award
The Lancashire Children's Book of the Year is awarded for a work of fiction suitable for the 11–14 age group. The judging panel consists entirely of 11–14-year-old pupils from secondary schools in Lancashire.

Past winners included *Chandra* by Frances Mary Hendry and *The Electric Kid* by Garry Kilworth.

Mind-Boggling Book Awards

This award's aim is to promote children's books which are accessible to children in both content and price – the entries must be in paperback and offer a gripping read. The judges are six children aged 9–12 and they choose from a shortlist of six titles selected by W H Smith children's book department.

Past winners include *Memoirs of a Dangerous Alien* by Maggie Prince and *Walk Two Moons* by Sharon Creech.

Mother Goose Award

The Mother Goose Award is presented annually by Books for Children Book Club to the Most Exciting Newcomer to Children's Book Illustration.

Past winners include *When Martha's Away* by Ingman Bruce and *I Love Animals* by Flora McDonnell.

NASEN Special Education Needs Award

This prize is awarded to a book which enhances the knowledge and understanding of those engaged in the education of children with special needs.

Past winners include *How to Write Really Badly* by Anne Fine and *The Golden Bird* by Berlie Doherty.

The Newbery Medal

This is an important American award given annually for the most distinguished contribution to American literature for children.

Past winners include *The Midwife's Apprentice* by Karen Cushman and *The Giver* by Lois Lowry.

The Science Book Prize

This prize is awarded for a popular non-fiction science and technology book suitable for the under-16's, which is judged to contribute to the public understanding of science.

Past winners include *The World of Weather* by Chris Maynard and *The Most Amazing Pop-up Science Book* by Jay Young.

Sheffield Children's Book Award

The Sheffield Children's Book Award is presented annually to the book chosen as the most enjoyable by the children of Sheffield.

There are three category winners and in 1996 the 7–11 and Overall Winner was *Double Act* by Jacqueline Wilson, the 12+ Category Winner went to *Unbeliever* by Robert Swindells and the 0–6 Category Winner went to *The Last Noo Noo* by Jill Murphy.

Signal Poetry Award

This award is intended to honour excellence in children's poetry.

Past winners include *Secrets* by Helen Dunmore and *Buns for Elephants* by Mike Harding.

Smarties Book Prize

This award was established to encourage high standards and stimulate interest in books for children. Children play a part in the judging process and from 1996 there has been a Gold, Silver and Bronze Award for three winning entries in each age category.

The Gold Award Winners in 1996 were, in the 9–11 category, *The Firework-Maker's Daughter* by Philip Pullman, in the 6–8 category, *The Butterfly Lion* by Michael Morpurgo and in the 0–5 category *Oops!* by Colin McNaughton.

TES Information Book Awards

The Times Educational Supplement (TES) Information Book Awards are given for distinction in content of information books. There is a junior award for a non-fiction title for children up to the age of 9, and a senior award for ages 10–16.

Joint senior winners in 1996 were *Young Citizen's Passport*, the Citizenship Foundation and *Keeping Clean* by Daisy Kerr, and the junior winner was *Children Just Like Me* by Barnabas and Anabel Kindersley.

Whitbread Children's Book of the Year

This award is for a book for children aged 7+.

Past winners include *The Tulip Touch* by Anne Fine and *The Wreck of Zanzibar* by Michael Morpurgo.

Bibliography

Adams, Richard, *Watership Down* (Puffin)

Atkins, Jill, *Jake the Snake* (Heinemann)

Awdry, Rev. W., *Thomas the Tank Engine* series (Reed/Heinemann)

Bierman, Valerie (ed.), *Best of Friends* (Methuen)

Bierman, Valerie (ed.), *Snake on the Bus* (Mammoth)

Blackman, Malorie, *Betsey's Birthday Surprise* (Piccadilly Press)

Blackman, Malorie, *Hacker* (Doubleday)

Blackman, Malorie, *Not So Stupid!* (Women's Press)

Blackman, Malorie and James, Rhian Nest, *That New Dress* (Simon & Schuster)

Blake, Jon, *How I Became a Star and Other Homework Excuses* (Viking)

Blyton, Enid, *Noddy* series (BBC)

Bradman, Tony (ed.), *A Sack of Story Poems* (Doubleday)

Breslin, Theresa, *Whispers in the Graveyard* (Methuen)

Bruse, Ingham *When Martha's Away* (Methuen)

Burgess, Melvin, *Junk* (Puffin)

Cameron, Ann, *The Stories Huey Tells* (Victor Gollancz)

Carroll, Lewis, *Alice in Wonderland* (Puffin)

Cave, Kathryn, and Riddell, Chris, *Something Else* (Viking)

Cole, Babette, *Drop Dead* (Jonathan Cape)

Cole, Babette, *Mummy Laid an Egg!* (Jonathan Cape)

Cole, Babette, *Princess Smartypants* (Puffin)

Cooney, Caroline B., *Freeze Tag* (Scholastic)

Cooper, Susan, *The Dark is Rising* (Puffin)

Coppard, Yvonne, *Don't Let it Rain* (Piccadilly Press)

Creech, Sharon, *Walk Two Moons* (Piper)

Cushman, Karen, *The Midewife's Apprentice* (Clarion Books)

Dahl, Roald, *Matilda* (Puffin)

Dale, Elizabeth, *Scrumpy* (Anderson)

Daniels, Lucy, *Animal Ark* series (Hodder Headline)

Dann, Colin, *Animals of Farthing Wood* (BBC)

Diaz Jovanovich, David and Bunting, Eve, *Smoky Night* (Harcourt Brace)

Dobson, Mary, *Roman Aromas*, Smelly Old History series (OUP)

Dobson, Mary, *Tudor Odours*, Smelly Old History series (OUP)

Dobson, Mary, *Victorian Vapours*, Smelly Old History series (OUP)

Doherty, Berlie, *Dear Nobody* (Lions)

Doherty, Berlie, *The Golden Bird* (Heinemann)

Drabble, Margaret, *The Millstone* (Penguin)

Dudman, Clare, *Edge of Danger* (Penguin)

Dunlop, Eillen, *Castle Gryffe* (Viking)

Dunmore, Helen, *Secrets* (Bodley Head)

Farman, John, *The Very Bloody History of Britain Without the Boring Bits* (Bodley Head)

Fine, Anne, *Bill's New Frock* (Mammoth)

Fine, Anne, *Crummy Mummy and Me* (Puffin)

Fine, Anne, *Flour Babies* (Puffin)

Fine, Anne, *Goggle Eyes* (Puffin)

Fine, Anne, *How to Write Really Badly* (Methuen)

Fine, Anne, *Madame Doubtfire* (Puffin)

Fine, Anne, *The Tulip Touch* (Puffin)

Finn Garner, James, *Politically Correct Bedtime Stories* (Souvenir Press)

French, Vivian, *Princess Primrose* (Walker Books)

Friel, Maeve, *Distant Voices* (Poolbeg)

Gaarder, Jostein, *Sophie's World* (Phoenix House)

Goldman, Jane, *Four Weddings, A Funeral and When You Can't Flush the Loo: Teenage Tips and Tactics* (Piccadilly Press)

Gordon, John, *Gilray's Ghost* (Walker Books)

Gowar, Mick, *Jimmy Woods and the Big Bad Wolf* (Puffin)

Grahame, Kenneth, *The Wind in the Willows* (Methuen)

Handford, Martin, *Where's Wally* series (Walker Books)

Harding, Mike, *Buns for Elephants* (Viking)

Hargreaves, Roger, *Mr Men* series (World International)

Harvey, John, *What About Sharon?* (Puffin)

Haugard, Eric, *Best of Books for Keeps* (Bodley Head)

Henderson, Kathy and Benson, Patrick *The Little Boat* (Walker Books)

Hendry, Frances Mary, *Chandra* (OUP)

Hill, Eric, *Spot* series (Puffin)

Hinton, S.E., *The Outsiders* (HarperCollins)

Hooper, Mary, *The Boyfriend Trap* (Walker Books)

Horse, Harry, *The Last Polar Bears* (Viking)

Howarth, Lesley, *Maphead* (Walker Books)

Hunter, Mollie, *A Pistol in Greenyards* (Canongate)

Hutchins, Pat, *Rosie's Walk* (Puffin)

Jones, Maurice, *I'm Going on a Dragon Hunt* (Puffin)

Kelly, John, and Burnie, Davie and Obin, *Everday Machines* (Hamlyn)

Kemp, Gene, *James Bodger and the Priory Ghost* (Puffin)

Kempton, Linda, *The naming of William Rutherford* (Mammoth)

Kerr, Daisy, *Keeping Clean* (Watts)

Kilworth, Garry, *The Electric Kid* (Transworld)

Kindersley, Barnabas and Anabel, *Children Just Like Me* (Dorling Kindersley)

King-Smith, Dick, *Clever Duck* (Viking)

King-Smith, Dick, *The Sheep Pig* (Puffin)

Knowles, Chris and Horsey, Julian, *The Paper Shoe Book* (Ebury Press)

Kraus, Robert, *Owliver* (Puffin)

Lawrence, Louise, *Children of the Dust* (Red Fox)

Lee, Rob, *Fireman Sam* series (Heinemann)

Lewis, C. S., *The Chronicles of Narnia* series (Collins)

Lewis, Sian, *Project Kite* (Red Fox)

Lowry, Lois, *The Giver* (Houghton)

Lynch, J. P., *The Christmas Miracle of Jonathan Toomey* (Walker Books)

Macphail, Catherine, *Run, Zan, Run* (Puffin)

MacRae, Lindsay, *You Canny Shove Yer Granny Off a Bus!* (Viking)

Magorian, Michelle, *Goodnight Mister Tom* (Puffin)

Mahy, Margaret, *The Other Side of Silence* (Hamish Hamilton)

Mahy, Margaret, *Tingleberries, Tuckertubs and Telephones* (Hamish Hamilton)

Maynard, Chris, *The World of Weather* (Kingfisher)

McDonnell, Flora, *I Love Animals* (Walker Books)

McNaughton, Colin, *Oops!* (Andersen)

Milne, A. A., *The House at Pooh Corner* (Mammoth)

Milne, A. A., *Winnie the Pooh* (Mammoth)

Moon and Moon, *Spinechillers: Ghosts,* Quids for Kids series (Harrap)

Morpurgo, Michael, *The Butterfly Lion* (Collins)

Morpurgo, Michael, *The Wreck of the Zanzibar* (Methuen)

Morpurgo, Michael (ed.), *Muck and Magic: Stories from a Countryside* (Mammoth)

Murphy, Jill, *The Last Noo Noo* (Walker Books)

O'Shea, Pat, *The Hounds of the Morrigan* (Puffin)

Ojeda, Linda, *I looked in the Mirror and Screamed: Healthier Eating for Teenagers* (Piccadillly Press)

Paul, Korky, and Thomas, Valerie, *Winnie the Witch* (OUP)

Pike, Christopher, *The last Vampire* (Hodder Headline)

Pilling, Ann, *Henry's Leg* (Puffin)

Pirani, Felix, *Abigail at the Beach* (Collins)

Postgate, Daniel, *Kevin Saves the World* (David Bennett Books)

Prince, Maggie, *Memoirs of a Dangerous Alien* (Orion)

Pullman, Philip, *Northern Lights* (Scholastic)

Pullman, Philip, *The Firework-Maker's Daughter* (Yearling)

Rathman, Peggy, *Office Buckle and Gloria* (Putnam)

Rees, Celia, *Colour Her Dead* (Pan)

Ridley, Philip, *Kasper in the Glitter* (Puffin)

Ridley, Philip, *Krindlekrax* (Red Fox)

Ridley, Philip, *The Meteorite Spoon* (Puffin)

Roche, Hannah and Pratt, Pierre, *Pete's Puddle*, My First Weather Book series (De Agostini)

Roche, Hannah and Pratt, Pierre, *Suki's Sun Hat*, My First Weather Book series (De Agostini)

Rogers, Gregory, *Way Home* (Anderson)

Rosen, Billi, *Andi's War* (Faber and Faber)

Rushton, Rosie, *Staying Cool, Surviving School: Secondary School Strategies* (Piccadilly Press)

Scott, Hugh, *The Place Between* (Walker Books)

Sefton, Catherine, *The Kidnapping of Suzie Q* (Puffin)

Smirthwaite, John, *Falcon's Quest* (Hodder)

Snow, Alan, Batt, Nick and Furlow, David, *PAWS* (HarperCollins)

Stevens, Roger, *The Howen* (Puffin)

Storr, Catherine, *Clever Polly and the Stupid Wolf* (Puffin)

Strachan, Ian, *The Stray Cat's Tale* (Heinemann)

Strong, Jeremy, *The Karate Princess* (Puffin)

Swindells, Robert, *Stone Cold* (Hamish Hamilton)

Swindells, Robert, *Unbeliever* (Hamish Hamilton)

Symes, Ruth, *The Master of Secrets* (Puffin)

Thompson, Pat (ed.), *A Bus Full of Stories for Four Year Olds* (Corgi)

Yolkien, J. R. R., *The Lord of the Rings* (HarperCollins)

Townsend, Sue, *The Secret Diary of Adrian Mole, Aged Thirteen and Three Quarters* (Mammoth)

Trivizas, Eugene, and Oxenbury, Helen *The Three Little Wolves and the Big Bad Pig* (Puffin)

Umansky, Kaye, *The Romantic Giant* (Hamish Hamilton)

Ure, Jean, *A Place to Scream* (Corgi)

Ure, Jean, *The Unknown Planet* (Walker Books)

Vail, Rachel, *Do-Over* (Mammoth)

Walsh, Jill Paton, *A Parcel of Patterns* (Puffin)

Waugh, Sylvia, *The Mennyms* (Julia MacRae)

Wegner, Fritz, *Heaven on Earth* (Walker Books)

Welford, Sue, *Night after Tomorrow* (OUP)

West, Colin, *Monty, the Dog Who Wears Glasses* (A&C Black)

Westall, Robert, *The Watch House* (Macmillan)

Whybrow, Ian, *The Little Wolf's Book of Badness* (Collins)

Williams, Jay, *The Practical Princess* (Hippo Books)

Wilson, Clive, *The Living Forests* (Kingfisher)

Wilson, Jacqueline, *Double Act* (Doubleday)

Wynne Jones, Diana, *A Tale of Time City* (Mammoth)

Young, Jay, *The Most Amazing Pop-up Science Book* (Watts)

Zindel, Paul, *I Never Loved Your Mind* (Red Fox)

CD-ROMS

Magic Tales (Ablac)
PAWS: A Personal Automated Wagging System (Domestic Funk/Virgin Records)
Eyewitness Virtual Reality (Dorling Kindersley)
Jungle Book (Electronic Arts)
Peter Rabbit's Interactive World (Frederick Warne)
The Adventures of Hyperman (IBM)
A Christmas Story (OUP)
Dragons (OUP)
The Fish Who Could Wish (OUP)
Winnie the Witch (OUP)

Magazines, Catalogues and Reference Works

100 Best Books: The Big Stories for Children, annual, (Young Book Trust)
Books for Keeps, 6 issues, annual subscription (Books for Keeps)
Carousel – The Guide to Children's Books, 3 issues, annual subscription (Carousel)
The Children's Book Handbook (Young Book Trust)
The Children's Bookseller, quarterly (J. Whitaker & Sons)
Dillon's Guide to Children's Books, annual, (Dillons)
The Fiction Writer's Handbook (Piatkus)
Novelist's Guide (Piatkus)
Our Choice 3: Good Reads Recommended by Teenagers for Teenagers (Young Book Trust)
Poetry: A Penguin Booklist (Penguin)
Waterstone's Guide to Children's Books, (Waterstone's)
The Writers' and Artists' Yearbook, (A&C Black)
The Writers' Handbook, (Macmillan)
Writers' News, monthly (Writers' News Limited)
Writing Magazine, bi-monthly, (Writers' News Limited)
Young Citizen's Passport, (Hodder Headline

INDEX